Work Hazards and
Industrial Conflict

Published for University of Rhode Island
by University Press of New England
Hanover, New Hampshire and London, England 1981

Work Hazards and Industrial Conflict

Carl Gersuny

University Press of New England

Sponsoring Institutions

Brandeis University

Clark University

Dartmouth College

University of New Hampshire

University of Rhode Island

Tufts University

University of Vermont

Copyright © 1981 by The Regents,
University of Rhode Island
All rights reserved
Library of Congress Catalog Card Number 80-51506
International Standard Book Number 0-87451-189-5
Printed in the United States of America

To Bridget Linehan

Contents

Tables

What mean ye that ye beat my people to pieces and grind the faces of the poor? saith the Lord God of Hosts.

Isaiah 3 : 15

Preface

BETWEEN the beaters and the beaten, the grinders and the ground, there is a fundamental clash of interests that goes to the heart of social inequality. As Phelps Brown put it: "It was still the worker whose bones were broken; the employers and shareholders had only to pay a premium. Industrial injuries remained a mark in the differences in privilege and status between employer and employed."[1] These differences in privilege and status give rise to a clash of interests between those whose health and longevity are impaired disproportionately in the work environment and those who control that environment and its reward structure.

The extent to which industrial hazards exist today has been pointed out by Ralph Nader: As "a form of violence, job casualties are statistically at least three times more serious than street crime, and with each new discovery, or documentation of a hitherto neglected exposure to gases, chemicals, particulates, radiation, or noise, the epidemic looms larger and more pervasive."[2] The risks of work injury and occupational disease are unequally distributed, and it is the manual workers most at risk who have a crucial interest in improving safety conditions. Their resistance to exploitation in this regard and the conditions of exploitation are central to the study of class structure.

Occupational safety and health are prominent concerns at present. Controversy exists over safety legislation and its enforcement, injury and compensation, as well as over health hazards and the cost of their abatement. Since its enactment, the Occupational Safety and Health Act of 1970 has been debated at length in the public media. Yet treatment of workers as an expendable factor of production to be discarded once incapacitated by work injury or occupational disease is nothing new but has received critical attention from the earliest days of industrial production.

This book is a study of the ongoing clash of opposing interests in the context of a changing legal framework. Despite apparently dramatic changes in the workplace, the conflict over work hazards has been a strong thread of continuity from the earliest days of industrial production to the present. Emergence of new hazards follows abatement of old ones, while conflict persists over the allocation of funds for prevention of industrial accidents and for meeting the cost of compensating casualties. These conflicts are examined by comparing material from the decades around the beginning of the twentieth century with data from the 1970s. The material from 1890 to 1910 is mainly from manuscript sources, while the more recent information was furnished by agencies of government, unions, and employers. Chapter 1 sets forth some pertinent concepts to relate the issue of industrial conflict over work hazards to the broader questions of class and class conflict. The second chapter describes the climate of industrial hazards in the United States around the turn of the century. Chapters 3 and 4 analyze accident records and correspondence from a number of now defunct New England textile mills, and data from these sources shed light on hitherto concealed machinations of the workplace. Chapter 5 briefly sketches the basic social reforms pertaining to work hazards enacted in the United States from 1910 to 1970 and culminating in the Occupational Safety and Health Act. The last chapter deals with recent patterns of conflict over safety and health issues of the workplace.

I acknowledge with gratitude the help I received in the preparation of this work, above all the unfailing kindness of Robert Lovett, manuscript curator of Baker Library at Harvard University. Staff members at the University of Rhode Island Library, the Fall River Public Library, the University of Lowell Library, the Countway Library, the Rhode Island Historical Society Library, the Merrimack Valley Textile Museum Library, and the State House Library in Boston were consistently helpful. For permitting access to the 1899–1905 register of Lowell Corporation Hospital I wish to thank Sister Yvette Thibaudeau, administrator of St. Joseph's Hospital in Lowell. The press and information section of the French Embassy kindly provided material on Roland Wuillaume's fatal accident. Eula Bingham, Assistant Secretary of Labor for Occupational Safety and Health, furnished valuable information, as did New Hampshire Labor Commissioner Robert M. Duvall. Helpful replies to inquiries were received from Bethlehem Steel Corporation, General Motors Corporation, Republic Steel Corporation, and Firestone Tire and Rubber Company, as well as from the United Mineworkers, United Automobile Workers, United Steelworkers and Textile Workers unions.

Portions of this book appeared in *Business History Review* (Autumn 1977), *Labor History* (Summer 1979), *New England Quarterly* (December 1979), and *Labor Studies Journal* (Fall 1980), by whose permission they appear here.

I am grateful to the University of Rhode Island for granting a sabbatical leave in the spring of 1975 during which this project was begun and for conditions of employment subsequent to that leave that made possible its completion. The research committee of my university defrayed the cost of typing the first draft and the overhead committee of the Department of Sociology, the second. This work benefitted enormously from the ministrations of an exemplary editor, Barbara Ras. My loyal spouse requested omission of the usual uxorious praise and I am pleased to comply.

This book is dedicated to Bridget Linehan, a textile worker whose mill manager wrote to the liability insurer after a 1908 work injury that he "tried to beat her down, but . . . she would not take a cent less" than her lost wages and medical expenses.[3]

CHAPTER 1

A Part of the Class Struggle

JUDGE Patrice de Charette, a French magistrate, created a sensation in 1975 when he went, accompanied by a deputy, to arrest and imprison the plant manager of a tar refinery where a worker had been killed in an industrial accident. The magistrate observed that he "would not be surprised if this case was discussed as part of the 'class struggle.'" His observation epitomizes the theme of this study, namely, how work hazards and the contention over the cost of prevention or compensation for injuries become elements of class conflict. The case raised to prominence by this dramatic judicial intervention began on January 23, 1975, when Roland Wuillaume died after his chest was crushed between two railroad cars at the refinery in Bethune, France. Judge de Charette said that he jailed the plant manager because he "considered the executive's negligence tantamount to premeditated murder." After six days in prison, the manager was released by order of a higher court, and when the case came to trial he received a fine and a suspended jail sentence of four to six months. Higher authorities denounced Judge de Charette for having "impaired the impartiality" of French justice, but he insisted, "I don't see why it is less serious to let men die at work than it is to steal a car."[1]

After eight workers at an Italian chemical plant died of bladder cancer resulting from exposure to toxic substances in the workplace, a court in Turin sentenced for manslaughter two owners, two managers, and the company doctor to prison terms ranging from three to six years. It was a landmark case since for the first time labor unions were involved as co-plaintiffs.[2]

After six workers were killed and thirty-nine injured by an explosion in a New York chewing gum factory, the corporation and four of its executives were indicted for reckless manslaughter and criminally negligent homicide; the indictments were later dismissed for insufficient evidence by a state supreme court justice. The district attorney had charged the company with ignoring the warnings of its own safety department, but the defense had argued that the indictments were an "unjustifiable misuse of the criminal process."[3]

Evidence that this type of conflict takes place under state socialism and is not limited to capitalist property relations comes from Hungary, where four managers received prison sentences ranging from one and one-half to three years after a foundry explosion killed nine workers.[4] Class conflict of a different sort was reported from the Soviet Union in the case of Vladimir Klebanov, who was committed to a psychiatric hospital in response to his complaints about coal mining hazards. He had attributed the high rate of mine fatalities and injuries in the Donets coal fields where he was employed to workers' fatigue resulting from pressure to increase production and from the imposition of double shifts. In China, during the last years of Mao, "strict observance of . . . safety measures was considered 'bourgeois' and cowardly." However, a 1979 oil rig accident that killed seventy-two workers has brought attention to "hazards which would put a Western industrialist out of business." Chinese Petroleum Ministry officials who claimed that "accidents are to be expected in the industry just as casualties are expected in wartime" were censured.[5]

The examples cited above involving criminal prosecution in several industrial societies are both dramatic and unusual. The ongoing adversary processes focused on safety and health hazards in the workplace usually are played out away from the criminal courts and, ordinarily, away from the spotlight of public attention. These adversary processes are very much a part of class conflict, as it is the intent of this book to demonstrate.

CLASS SITUATION

Before proceeding to explore this proposition, it is appropriate to define some terms, particularly since there is much debate over definitions of class, exploitation, class conflict, and class consciousness.

To say that Roland Wuillaume faced a much higher probability of being killed in the tar refinery at Bethune than was faced by the owners or by the plant manager is to state a truism that goes to the very heart of the question of class inequality. There are more casualties among the "hands" on the shop floor than in the front office or the boardroom. Along with differences in power and privilege, differences in the hazards to life and limb characterize class divisions in society. These class divisions originated with the emergence of a division of labor between manual or material labor on the one hand and nonmanual or mental labor on the other.

Language reflects the reality of material labor, as in the Greek word for work, *ponos*, which has the same root as the Latin word for sorrow, *poena*. *Poena* also means penalty, reflecting the ancient tradition that work is a penalty for original sin and that penitentiaries are places of sorrow where work is done. The French *travailler*, to work, is derived from a Latin word referring to a kind of torture.[6]

In the earliest stages of technological development, these pains and tortures were borne by all in the struggle for survival. The implements at hand were not sufficiently productive to yield a surplus, accounting for the fact that hunting and gathering societies were generally the most egalitarian. Technological advances have served not only to make human agents more efficient, but to create marked inequalities as to how the pains of manual labor are distributed in society.

Max Weber defined the class situation as "the typical probability of procuring goods, gaining position in life and finding inner satisfaction" based on "control over goods and skills and from their income-producing uses within a given economic order," that is, on market capabilities in capital markets, labor markets, and commodity markets. "In principle," wrote Weber, "the various controls over consumer goods, means of production, assets, resources and skills each constitute a *particular* class situation."[7] Class situation is the source of the life chances of members of society. By life chances, Weber meant, "the typical chance for a supply of goods, external living conditions, and personal life experiences, insofar as this chance is determined by the amount and kind of power, or lack of such, to dispose of goods and skills for the sake of income in a given economic order."[8] Employment in a hazardous occupation and the contingencies attendant upon such employment can thus reasonably be viewed as central to questions of class in Weberian terms. Work injury and occupational disease impair market capacities for future earnings and impair life chances, which include chances for health and survival.

Tawney wrote that the material wealth which renews society is "hewn daily in the gloom of the mine and fashioned unceasingly in the glare of the forge; and both the hierarchy of the world of leisure and the hierarchy of productive effort" are characterized by "the separation of the groups which organize, direct and own the material apparatus of industry from those which perform its routine work."[9] The hazards encountered in the gloom of the mine and in the glare of the forge are central to the inequality of life chances which Weber described.

"Class is defined by men as they live their own history, and, in the end this is its only definition," wrote E. P. Thompson. Class, in his view, "is something which in fact happens (and can be shown to have happened) in human relationships."[10] The most salient relationships in shaping this experience of class are in the sphere of production, which is characterized, among other things, by a patently unequal distribution of hazards. This unequal distribution of work injury and occupational disease is part and parcel of the pattern of exploitation typical of production in hierarchic social structures. What is meant by exploitation (as a sociological rather than an economic concept) must be discussed.

In a variety of sociological traditions, exploitation is a concept that refers to unequal exchange. For example, Durkheim wrote that "common morality very severely condemns every kind of leonine contract wherein one of the parties is exploited by the other."[11] E. A. Ross defined it as "any regular profiting of one element in society at the expense of other elements, which would be abolished if the element came to be equal in power."[12] In order to assuage the uneasiness among some sociologists about using the term exploitation, Gouldner suggests the tongue-in-cheek euphemism "reciprocity imbalance" to take its place.[13]

Ruyle wrote that social classes are "populations interacting in a predator–prey relationship." In this relationship there is a net energy flow from an exploited to an exploiting class. In other words, energy expended in the labor process by one class accrues to another class.[14] In Ruyle's view the "ruling class is a predator population" that manipulates the system of exploitation to maximize the inflow of energy from the subordinate classes. He holds this to be "analogous to predator–prey relationships between animal species, except that the stakes are not the food energy locked up in animal flesh, but the ethnoenergy the human animal can expend in production."[15] Intraspecies predation is *cannibalism*, and though Ruyle qualifies his analogy, in industry, the consuming of human bodies in the work process can be viewed as a sort of *metaphoric cannibalism*. Bodies are destroyed or impaired by work hazards whose abatement would entail costs that the predators wish to avoid.

Differences in work situation with respect to safety and health hazards go to the heart of the subject of exploitation.

Work relations are defined in terms of a wage bargain and an effort bargain, each of which characteristically subjects workers to exploitive disadvantages because of the disparities in power. These disparities in power rest on property relations in which workers are dependent for their livelihood upon employers who dispose of instruments of production. It is this dependence that confers power on employers, a power that is relative to the number of alternative opportunities that are available to the workers. Part of the work situation and a consideration in the effort bargain is the wear and tear suffered by the worker.

CLASS CONSCIOUSNESS

"Few things are more difficult to establish than class consciousness,"[16] wrote a historian of the industrial revolution in England, a country in which existence of class consciousness may be proved more readily than in the United States. Notwithstanding its elusiveness, questions about class consciousness are inevitably raised in connection with studies of class conflict. Three characteristics have been identified as necessary ingredients of class consciousness among workers: (1) perception of an identity of interests with one's fellow workers; (2) recognition of an adversary relationship with another class; and (3) definition of class conflict not only as being fundamental to all other relationships, but as portending an alternative social order.[17] Hobsbawm points out, however, that the absence of these characteristics "does not imply the absence of classes and class conflict."[18] What sort of class conflict can manifest itself in the absence of class consciousness and what alternatives to class consciousness serve as its motivation?

Thompson writes about the "temptation to suppose that class is a thing . . . 'It,' the working class, is assumed to have a real existence, which can be defined almost mathematically— so many men who stand in a certain relation to the means of production. Once this is assumed it becomes possible to deduce the class-consciousness which 'it' ought to have (but seldom does have) if 'it' was properly aware of its own position and real interests."[19]

There obviously has to be some sort of consciousness as a prerequisite for conflict, but what sort of consciousness? There has to be a recognition that one's interests are being impaired by an adversary, that one is being thwarted or diminished in a way that is not inevitable, but for which some identifiable person or group is responsible.

Individualism—in a sense, the very antithesis of class consciousness—can provide the motivational basis for class conflict, because it casts man as "a receptacle of interest."[20] The class position of the individual shapes his most fundamental interests, whether he thinks about class or not. It is thus possible to explain resistance to exploitation in general and to inordinate risk to one's body from work hazards in particular, by reference to Bentham rather than to Marx. Bentham argued that anyone "enjoying a certain *good*, i.e. a certain *pleasure* or *exemption* from pain" has "*an interest* in the possession of that same good" and an "*aversion* to the idea of not possessing it."[21] If it is true, as Bentham claims, that "every body of men is governed altogether by its conception of what is its interest in the narrowest and most selfish sense of the word interest," then those who are subjected to the *pain* of work injury and occupational disease have a strong motive for resistance. Individualism casts workers as "proprietors of themselves" with a right to convey their capacity to labor,[22] and work hazards impair their proprietary interests in their own persons.

Individualism is a state of mind found in societies where "little respect is paid to tradition or authority,"[23] because tradition and authority thwart individual initiative. The spread of individualism to propertyless workers undermines deference and submissiveness. Dawley wrote that the impact of individualism and egalitarianism in the United States generated worker hostility toward "inequality and authoritarianism in the management of American industry. . . . The very historical conditions that gave rise to individualism created a class system in which individualism became the basis for collective action of one class against another. In any marketplace transaction, buyers and sellers have opposing interests. As buyers of labor, manufacturers had a common interest among themselves which was opposed to the common interest of workers, as sellers."[24]

To be a proprietor of oneself with an interest in avoiding pain, however, would not suffice to generate resistance to those who inflict pain. Barrington Moore argued that "people are evidently inclined to grant legitimacy to anything that is or seems to be inevitable, no matter how painful it may be. . . . The conquest of this sense of inevitability is essential to the development of politically effective moral outrage. For this to happen, people must perceive and define their situation as the consequence of human injustice: a situation that they need not, cannot, and ought not to endure." Denial of the legitimacy of suffering occurs when "causes of misery appear to the sufferers as due to the acts of identifiable superiors."[25] Thus we shall see that the individualist premises of the common law gave rise to a class of individual employee plaintiffs and litigation against a class of employer defendants. "The common thread woven into all torts is the idea of unreasonable interference with the interests of others."[26] In short, litigiousness is not class consciousness, but where the plaintiffs are in one class and the defendants in another, litigation is a form of class conflict.

Behavior—in Maslow's view—may be seen in terms of response to a *hierarchy of needs.*[27] If the most compelling needs are met, the next level in the hierarchy of needs comes into motivational focus. The highest ranked needs fall in the category of physiological needs, followed by safety needs, needs for affection, esteem (including self-esteem), and realization of one's potential. The fact that safety needs rank second only to the physiological needs to maintain the chemical balance of the body, that is, to offset hunger, thirst, and fatigue, underscores the importance of industrial safety and health.

CLASH OF INTERESTS

Two kinds of interests are distinguished by Wright, immediate and fundamental. The former "constitute[s] interests within a given structure of social relations," and the latter, "interests which call into question the structure of social relations itself."[28] The so-called fundamental class interests exist in the minds of those imbued with a socialist class consciousness, while the immediate interests—those which take the existing property relations as "given" and seek a "better deal" within that framework—require no class consciousness at all. They require only that the subordinate be able to define his situation in ways that are at variance with the definitions of the owners, managers, and overseers to whose authority he is subjected.

Opposition of interests between those who dominate the process of production and those who are dependent upon them is inherent in the class structure, and any adversary encounter based on such divergence of interests is a manifestation of class conflict. The judicial proceedings in connection with the fatalities described at the beginning of this chapter are part of what the French magistrate called the class struggle because clashes over issues of safety and health are as germane to the divergence of interests as disputes over the wage bargain. Nor should it be thought that class conflict is manifested only when the subordinate class puts up resistance against the dominant class. In Hobsbawm's view, "class struggle is normally fought or felt with much greater and more consistent bitterness on the bourgeois side." Exploitation and resistance to exploitation are elements of a potentially two-sided conflict, but lack of resistance does not imply absence of conflict.

Expressions of class conflict are vitually limitless. Crime has been called a sort of "unorganized class struggle," and authorities on voting behavior have referred to an election as a "democratic class struggle." A "refusal to understand" has been described by Hobsbawm as a form of class struggle.[29] Passive resistance, foot-dragging, and any inattention to authority by subordinates can be seen as a kind of latent class conflict.

In his discussion of different kinds of antagonism in the class structure, T. H. Marshall describes one that is particularly pertinent to the issue of safety in the workplace. It is the "conflict that arises over the division of labour . . . over the terms on which co-operation is to take place, as illustrated by a wage dispute between employer and employed."[30] This is a facet of class conflict that many writers refer to as *industrial conflict*, even though it was a feature of preindustrial societies as well.

Plantation slaves in the South, despite threats of whipping and other punishment, sought to shape the effort bargain in terms of limits consistent with their own interest.

> By moving only so fast and being willing to take some blows, they compelled even an overseer who used his whip with minimum provocation to adjust his sights. . . . Thus slaves struggled to influence their own working conditions. Their actions did not challenge slavery *per se*. . . . Yet in an important sense the slowdowns and resistance to overwork contributed more to the slaves' struggle for survival than did many bolder individual acts . . . to attack slavery itself.[31]

There are numerous examples of antagonism between workers and superiors. In peasant societies there is a perennial tug-of-war between those who cultivate and the outsiders who demand part of the product. The wage and effort bargains merge in the division of crops. In the manorial system in England after the Norman conquest, despite the overwhelming advantage of the rulers, every manor "was the scene of an endless contest in which lord and serf each struggled to obtain their own ends."[32] A similar picture emerges from Moslem India, where the contest is between "the administration and peasants, the former endeavoring to discover and appropriate what the latter endeavored to retain and conceal."[33] The conflict is dramatized by Chinese cultivators who were "experts at filling the containers of rice in such a way that they appear most liberally full when they are really partly empty."[34] In this case, covert resistance was adopted when there were no legitimate means of redress.

The reasons why conflict is inherent in hierarchic work situations are set forth by Clark Kerr in his analysis of the relationships between labor and management. First, he points to the inevitable discrepancy between wishes and fulfillment in an environment of scarcity, which means that the "desires of the parties are more or less unlimited, while the means of satisfaction are limited." The extent to which one group can achieve satisfaction affects the achievement potential of others. Secondly, the necessity for coordination results in situations in which "someone manages and someone is managed, and this is an eternal opposition of interest." Rapid social change is viewed as another source of conflict because "even if a certain distribution of income and power could be devised which, in a given situation was not subject to controversy . . . the situation itself would change."[35]

Overt or covert resistance is a factor in both servile and contractual work relationships. Under the latter, "disagreement as to the terms of cooperation is normal and chronic. It is implied in the bargaining process out of which the contract emerges."[36] If there were no divergence of interests, there would be no occasion to enter into a contract, which is, according to Durkheim, "only a truce, and very precarious; it suspends hostility only for a time."[37]

Behrend observed that a wage bargain and an effort bargain were part of every employment contract and that "workers will have an upper limit to the amount of exertion they will put out and employers a lower limit to the level of exertion that they will tolerate without firing the worker."[38] From this proposition it is but one step to the view that managerial attempts to elicit effort beyond the workers' upper limit or worker resistance that reduces effort beyond the employer's lower limit will occasion overt conflict. Without elaborating on the complexity of the link between the two bargains, it is also possible to state that the upper and lower limits of exertion may vary in relation to different levels of compensation. Assessment of the wage and effort bargains will be shaped according to whether the subject of the bargain is a cost or a benefit. Wages are a cost to the employer and a benefit for the employee. Conversely, labor effort is a cost to the worker and a benefit to the employer. These divergent definitions are wellsprings of class conflict. The ubiquity of conflict arising out of contrary interests is well established, irrespective of whether labor is performed in servile or contractual relationships, under industrial or preindustrial technology, or under feudal, capitalist, or state socialist property relations.

In industrial societies, the hierarchic division of labor generates a wide-ranging pattern of industrial conflict that includes, according to Kornhauser, "the total range of behavior and attitudes that express opposition and divergent orientations between industrial owners and managers on the one hand and working people and their organizations on the other hand."[39] This conflict is demonstrated by activities ranging from peaceful bargaining and grievance handling, to strikes, boycotts, political action, restriction of output, sabotage, absenteeism, and "such rigid adherence to the rules that output is restricted."[40]

Much of industry, as characterized by R. H. Tawney, "is carried on in the intervals of a disguised social war." This animosity should not be perceived as the consequence of a breakdown of communications. Rather, it is inherent in the conflict of interests between workers and managers.

The idea that industrial peace can be secured merely by the exercise of tact and forbearance is based on the idea that there is a fundamental identity of interest between the different groups engaged in it, which is occasionally interrupted by regrettable misunderstandings. Both the one idea and the other are an illusion. The disputes which matter are not caused by misunderstanding of identity of interests, but by a better understanding of diversity of interests.[41]

Similar conflict exists under state socialism. According to Wesolowski, "contradictions of interest in socialist countries can result in something resembling antagonistic contradiction, since overpayment and underpayment may be viewed as a particular form of 'exploitation' of some people by others."[42] In a study of Soviet industrial disputes, McAuley cites premium pay systems in which bonuses for managers were "dependent on economies in the wage fund," which meant managers wanted to minimize the wage bill and workers sought to maximize it.[43] Workers who seek to gain in the wage and effort bargain are stigmatized for harboring a capitalist spirit and seeking to give the state less work and to receive greater rewards. "The selfish demands of such people [and] their failure to fulfill their obligations produce labor disputes," according to a Soviet commentary.[44]

Braverman pointed out that although "the Soviet working population bears all the stigmata of the Western working classes,"[45] it must bear them without benefit of genuine trade union representation in the adversary processes which these stigmata entail. It follows that being exploited in a democratic capitalist society is less burdensome than being exploited in an undemocratic state socialist society that brooks no dissent from its myths of harmony.

What the worker receives for his pains and what he has to give are the key issues in wage bargain and effort bargain. These two sides of the coin are not unrelated, but they serve separately to generate conflict. Dobb points out that what interests the worker is "his earning in relation . . . to his output of physical energy or his bodily wear and tear . . . what he gets compared to what he gives."[46]

The worker gives in general terms the best years of his life. Under conditions detrimental to health and safety, the wear and tear on the worker is greater than that experienced by other more privileged groups. While labor is perishable, so is the laborer. A disproportionate number perish before their time because of adverse conditions. Since one's interest in avoiding injury, disease, and presenile death is beyond controversy, being subjected to disproportionate risks in the work environment is an occasion for resistance and conflict. There is, thus, a struggle for the elimination of health and safety hazards and for recompense in cases of inordinate wear and tear when these hazards take their toll.

WEAR AND TEAR

Adam Smith wrote that "though the wear and tear of a free servant be equally at the expense of his master, it costs him generally much less than that of a slave."[47] Because the master had an investment in his human chattel, he had to protect this investment in sickness and in health. In the free laborer, whose labor power is hired for a specified term, there is no such investment and no ongoing obligation during disability. As Dobb concludes, under such conditions the employer "may have less regard for the personal welfare of his workers than would be the case under a slave system."[48]

In Smith's view the expense for wear and tear should not merely provide for the individual disabled by excessive wear and tear, but that the total wage bill should permit "survival of the race of journeymen and servants, according as the increasing, diminishing or stationary demand of society may happen to require."[49] Disabled journeymen and servants had to shift for themselves. Presumably the wage had been sufficient to induce them to risk the hazards of employment, and the employer had no obligation to his worker beyond the term of employment, even if the employment was terminated because of an accident. This lesson was not lost on those slave owners, cited by Genovese, who took to manumitting disabled slaves in the years before the Emancipation Proclamation.[50]

The interest of the worker in minimizing the wear and tear he experiences in the course of his labors differs from the interest of the employer in minimizing the costs of preventive measures or compensation for injuries suffered. It follows then that industrial health hazards are at issue in industrial conflict as much as other facets of the effort bargain or the wage bargain.

The conflict over industrial safety legislation is of long

standing and is dramatized by the similarity between comments made by Karl Marx in 1871 and observations made 100 years later by U.S. Congressman James G. O'Hara. In discussing the revision of the British factory act, Marx pointed to the "fanatical opposition of the masters to those clauses which imposed on them a slight expenditure on appliances for protecting the limbs of their work people." These provisions constituted interference with what Marx called the "exploitary rights of capital."[51]

O'Hara, commenting in 1971 on passage on the Occupational Safety and Health Act, noted that "an unremitting effort has been made in the Congress, over . . . the opposition first of the business community and, then, of the Nixon Administration, to put effective occupational safety legislation on the statute books."[52] That the conflict over enactmeent was but a prelude to ongoing conflict over enforcement is illustrated by another echo of the 1871 scenario. A manual on health hazards in the work environment points out that under the 1970 law, "there are only about 500 inspectors for 4.1 million workplaces. . . . During the first eight months of the act, inspectors visited 17,743 workplaces. At this rate it would take them 230 years to visit all the workplaces in our country. Even if the number of inspectors were increased to the projected level for the year 2000, it would still take 46 years to inspect all workplaces once."[53]

Attacked from one side for promoting programs that are too costly for industry and from the other for doing too little to assure workers' health and safety, the Occupational Health and Safety Administration is a focal point of conflicting interests. This conflict is mirrored at the state and enterprise level in many ways, because the cost of establishing and maintaining a safe and healthful work environment is as much a source of industrial conflict as any other cost item.

Standards dealing with levels of vinyl chloride, asbestos, coal dust, and other hazardous substances are attacked by both sides as being too lenient on the one hand, or too restrictive on the other. Numerous cases of injury or disease pit the company doctor against the victim's family doctor as third parties in adversary proceedings. Refusal to work under what employees perceive as unsafe conditions evokes disciplinary penalties, which in turn lead to grievances and cases of arbitration. Injury awards and compensation rates are frequently assailed as too high or too low, depending upon whether they are cost items or income items. Thus the issues of health hazards epitomize Marshall's description of class conflict over the terms of cooperation.

Resistance to harmful conditions, refusal to work unless hazards are eliminated, the struggle over restitution as well as over legislation and its enforcement—these are basic processes of industrial conflict. In every case the parties to the work contract have divergent interests because the cost incurred by one side varies directly with the other side's benefits (for example, in the form of a safe and healthful work environment). So long as insufficient power is brought to bear in order to eliminate hazards, enterprises receive "a subsidy coined in blood, broken bones, broken health, physical pain, mental anguish and the ultimate trauma of death."[54]

This "subsidy" is inimical to the workers who provide it. Good health and longevity are desirable no less for the working class than for any other. Industrial conditions that impair health and shorten life are focal points of conflict within and without the enterprise. Within the enterprise, worker safety is a subject for negotiations at the bargaining table, and on the shop floor it presents occasions for strikes, slowdowns, grievances, absenteeism, and other forms of resistance. In the public arena industrial hazards engage the attention of reform movements; they become subjects of legislation and litigation, and in general, attract attention for those concerned with the general welfare. As Ray Davidson pointed out, "the fact is that the American system is an adversary system. . . . Under this adversary system, government regulations of health and safety conditions can be effective only if there is a force which aggressively presents the workers' views. Management will certainly resist regulations."[55]

Presented in the pages to follow is documentation of a shocking succession of industrial horrors and the treatment of industrial casualties. These cases inevitably raise questions about the ethics of employers and managers. Are there not enlightened enterprises whose leaders wish to treat workers in accordance with the Golden Rule? To cast the health and safety question in terms of good or evil individuals is to miss the whole point. Abatement of hazards inevitably entails costs and the hypothetical "good" management that pays the price for greater safety will be at a competitive disadvantage in relation to its "evil" rivals who refuse to pay that price. It is in this context that we see one of the manifestations of T. H. Marshall's category of intraclass conflict that has some bearing on this topic.

The issue is not a moral one but a political one. The imposition of the uniform health and safety standards that are needed for abatement of work hazards depends upon the marshalling of greater power by proponents of stringent legislation than by its adversaries. In the absence of legal constraints, humane and enlightened enterprises would face bankruptcy while cruel and self-serving ones would prosper. If the costs of hazard abatement and of compensation for casualties are higher in one jurisdiction than in another, a parade of runaway shops from the high-cost locality to the low-cost one would serve to validate this proposition. This is not to imply that the conflict over work hazards is devoid of an ethical dimension. Nor is it a conflict in which one side represents unmitigated evil while the other is a repository of pure virtue.

The need for compulsion to secure the curtailment of work hazards has been nowhere more clearly put forward than in a footnote of the appellate decision in *AFL-CIO* v. *Brennan*, a case involving safety standards for power presses:

Although many employers in all industries have demonstrated an exemplary degree of concern for health and safety in the workplace, their efforts are too often undercut by those who are not so concerned. Moreover, that fact is that many employers . . . simply cannot make the necessary investment in health and safety, and survive competitively, unless all are compelled to do so.[56]

The interests of regulated industries impel them to resist compulsion and keep it to a minimum, while the interests of the workers whom the regulations are intended to protect motivate efforts to maximize that compulsion.

This clash of interests may be viewed as a permanent source of conflict in hierarchic industrial societies, that is, all industrial societies, because the abatement of injury and disease arising from exposure to work hazards entails problems of cost allocation. The benefit of one side is a cost of the other, and costs are a factor to be minimized. In the final analysis, the conflict over work hazards is a conflict between the enterprise costs and the social costs of production. Social costs include "all direct and indirect losses suffered by third persons or the general public as a result of private economic activities . . . for which private entrepreneurs are not easily held accountable." One major thrust of reform legislation has been to prevent or compensate for the imposition of social costs, because in the absence of legal constraints, "private business would continue to shift part of the costs of production to society."[57] The most obvious sort of social cost is "the impairment of the physical and mental health of laborers in the course of the productive process."[58] It is in the interests of workers to avoid such impairment and to see to it that the costs of prevention and of actual losses remain costs of the enterprise. The entrepreneur, on the other hand, has an interest in minimizing his costs, in part by deflecting them on third parties, especially on the employees over whom he has power because they are dependent on continued employment for their livelihood. Thus the conflict is joined.

The effect of this conflict is an ongoing series of compromises, reflecting the relative power of the adversaries and prevailing public policy. The importance of law in channeling and mitigating the confrontation of unequal power groups is of great importance for this subject. The conflict over work hazards, perhaps more than any other facet of industrial conflict, is shaped by the political processes of legislation, law enforcement, and adjudication.

CHAPTER 2

More Dangerous Than War

"WAR IS safe compared to railroading in this country."
Gilbert Roe's characterization of railroad worker safety was an apt comment on overall working conditions during
the first decade of the twentieth century, the period during
which the toll from work injuries reached its peak. Another
commentator described those years as "dark ages when the
human machine was driven to the limit without lubrication or
repair or simply 'scrapped' when disease, often the direct result
of the occupation, robbed it of further usefulness."[1]

Worker fatalities on U.S. railroads reached a peak in 1904
with a rate of 28 per 10,000 employees, while the injury rate
reached a high point of one in ten employees in 1916. In turn,
railroading was "safe" compared with coal mining, an industry
in which the mortality rate from work accidents reached 48.1
per 10,000 workers in 1906. The average yearly death toll for
1900 to 1906 in the coal mines of the United States exceeded the
rates of major European coal-producing countries: per 10,000
workers the United States had 33.5 deaths; France, 9.1; Bel-
gium, 10.3; Great Britain, 12.9; and Prussia, 20.6.[2]

While much of the material in the present study of this period originates from the New England cotton textile industry,
which was "safer" than mining, railroading, or war, it sheds
light on the state of industrial health and safety during the
flood tide of industrialization. By focusing on the textile industry experience, it avoids vulnerability to the charge of gener-
alizing from extreme cases.

Health hazards to which cotton mill workers were subjected

included dust from the cotton itself, as well as from clay used in sizing, heat, long periods of standing, stooping posture, monotony of work, and strain upon attention, combined with excessive noise and vibration of machinery.

Citing a tabulation of diagnosed conditions among cotton operatives treated at the hospital in Preston, Lancashire, for a six-year period prior to 1892, which included 739 weavers and 676 in other mill classifications, Arlidge reported that 9.9 percent of weavers and 11.9 percent of the other operatives were diagnosed to have tuberculosis. The data also showed that 32.2 percent of the weavers and 31.3 percent of the other operatives were suffering from bronchitis. He concluded that the "special major evils of cotton manufacturing belong to the respiratory system."[3] Similar conditions will be documented below for New England cotton operatives.

Describing traumatic injury, Arlidge went on to say: "It is no wonder that accidents abound, considering the extent of machinery, the velocity of movement, the proximity of machines to each other, the loosely hanging gearing, and the liability to the loosing and flying off of some parts of the machine."[4]

The 1910 level of sanitation in the New England cotton mills is graphically documented in some of the congressional evidence published during this period. "The use in common of a single drinking cup is nearly universal,"[5] in the factories so that it is surprising that there were not more cases of typhoid fever and other infectious diseases.

The mills were veritable breeding grounds for the tubercle bacillus. Spitting and coughing by workers in various stages of tuberculosis, as well as the weaver's kiss of death (threading of shuttles by oral suction) spread tuberculosis with devastating results. The practice of spitting received particular attention. One Massachusetts health department report asserted: "No one can spend his or her working days in a room where others in incipient stages of consumption habitually spit upon the floor, without the gravest danger of acquiring the disease."[6] Nevertheless, in 46 New England cotton mills surveyed by the

U.S. Labor Department in 1906, spitting was found to be customary in 38 (82.6 percent), while cuspidors were provided in 17 mills (37 percent).[7] Ironically, Massachusetts state law at the same time prohibited spitting and required that cuspidors be provided.

The condition of toilets in the factories contributed to the general unsanitary environment.

The water closets in many mills have poor fixtures, which are in many cases broken, and receiving no attention they remain in a disgusting condition. . . . Some mill officials complain that their attempts to keep the water closets sanitary . . . receive little or no cooperation from the employees. . . . It is evident, on the other hand, that in many cases the conditions found can exist only as a result of the neglect of ordinary care on the part of those responsible.[8]

Other amenities taken for granted in later stages of industrialization were lacking. In 22 Massachusetts cotton mills none had a wash room or a dressing room for men, none had a dressing room for women, and only two had women's wash rooms. Among 46 New England mills only one had a lunch room separate from the work rooms and none had a rest room for employees.[9] Needless to say, these conditions were not conducive to sanitation.

In light of such conditions it may reasonably be asked what sort of medical services were available to workers who fell prey to the hazards of the industrial environment. According to L. J. Henderson the general level of available medical care was poor: "It was not until about the year 1910 or 1912 in the United States that a random patient with a random disease consulting a doctor chosen at random stood better than a 50–50 chance of benefitting from the encounter."[10] Given the obvious class differences affecting the receipt of medical services, there is every reason to suppose that the ministrations to the industrial casualties fell below even that level both on and off the job.

The quality of medical care delivered at the factory level during the period under study is nowhere more severely censured than in the writings of the pioneer physicians who strove to upgrade industrial medicine. Harry E. Mock, for many years the chief physician for Sears Roebuck and Company, wrote, "The old time company surgeon . . . as a rule rendered very inefficient service to the employees. His standing in the profession was of a very low average and the character of his work was of a low standard. He was a company surgeon in word and deed and too often was only on the side of the employer as represented by the insurance company."[11]

Mock had entered the field himself against the advice of one of his medical school professors who warned him to forget it. In his professor's opinion "the reputation of most company surgeons 'stunk to high heaven.'" At that time the Chicago Medical Society took the position that "company surgeons, with a few outstanding exceptions, were poorly qualified. They accepted such positions because they could not earn a living in regular practice. . . . These men took care only of minor injuries. When they attempted to treat a major injury, they usually 'messed up.'"[12]

Alice Hamilton, who became an industrial physician in 1910, also reported that at that time "for a surgeon or physician to accept a position with a manufacturing company was to earn the contempt of his colleagues as a 'contract doctor.'"[13] Another of the great pioneers in occupational medicine, David L. Edsall, suggested that the fault lay as much with the employers as with the company surgeons because, "there has been at times in the instructions under which they work so much 'benevolent feudalism' . . . that they have often not fully gained the confidence of the working people."[14] Edsall was undoubtedly a master of understatement, because the benevolence of the dispensation to which he refers was probably largely illusory, and far from fully gaining the confidence of the working people, company doctors were viewed as adversaries by their patient populations, as is the case in many situations even today.

Work injuries are more readily identified than occupational

diseases and more data are available on the former than on the latter. In one study analyzing accidents in 37 New England cotton mills during 1906 data showed that in 348 cases for which the duration of disability was reported, the average lost work time was 12.6 days. In the same study, the extent of aid to the victims was reported for 691 cases: in 556 (80.5 percent), only the cost of medical assistance was defrayed by the employer; in 80 cases (11.6 percent) no aid or compensation was furnished; lump sum payments were given in 35 cases (5.1 percent); while in only 20 injuries (2.8 percent) were full or half wages paid.[15]

In a study of the Pacific Mills at Lawrence, Massachusetts from August 1900 to July 1905, 1,000 accidents were analyzed including 2 fatalities, 86 serious injuries, 910 slight injuries, and 2 unclassified. Among these casualties, 54.2 percent were employed in the mill less than one year and 62.7 were thirty years of age or younger. The actual causes and their incidence among the 1,000 injuries are as follows:[16]

Caught in machinery in operation in ordinary usage	320
Caught in machinery while cleaning contrary to orders	111
Careless handling of tools or implements of work	98
Handling machinery, merchandise, etc. in transportation	137
Slipped on floors, etc. and caught by machinery	61
Injured by trucks or wagons used in the work	36
Falls	47
Elevators	39
Injured by belts	32
Splinters	19
Flying shuttles	19
Other	81
	1000

Some mill departments presented greater risk of injury than others, as can be seen from the accident rates from various departments of the Pacific Mills given in Table I.

Among the nonproduction workers the yard and shop employees were in the most hazardous classifications. The same held true among production operatives for the pickers and strippers in the card rooms.

TABLE I. *Annual Accident Rates by Department, Pacific Mills, 1900–1905*

Department	Accident Rate per 1,000 Employees
Yard and stable	268.5
Picker rooms	227.3
Repair shops	113.6
Card strippers	113.5
Mule spinning	61.8
Frame tenders	49.4
Carding and roving	35.2
Weaving	20.8
Ring spinning	10.8

SOURCE: Massachusetts State Board of Health, *Thirty-Eighth Annual Report*, Boston: Wright & Potter, 1907, p. 480.

In the Pacific Mills study, based on company accident reports, the imputation of underlying causes is characterized by the prevailing managerial bias with respect to such matters.[17]

Underlying Cause	Number of Accidents
Careless manipulation	539
Deliberate carelessness	164
Inattention to surroundings	177
Carelessness of fellow workman	51
Unforeseen liability	60
Unclassified	9
	1000

The imputation of carelessness on the part of the victim or of a fellow worker in 93.1 percent of the Pacific Mills injury series was (and remains to this day) a fundamental tenet of managerial folklore.

A General Electric executive in a 1917 address to the cotton manufacturers association, expounded a callous view of industrial safety. "Is it not clear that the majority of accidents have their chief source in a spirit of carelessness?" His rhetoric ignored the realities of the industrial environment, and he asked,

"What kind of safeguard could we erect around a man who trips over his own shoe-lace . . . or who shakes a ladder with a man on it 'just for fun?'" This explanatory tour de force concluded with a digression into Social Darwinism and a suggestion that too many safety devices would render workers unfit for the struggle to survive: "Even if it were possible it would be unwise so to surround red-blooded human beings with safeguards as to convert them into such unthinking mollycoddles, while in the shop, that they would rush thoughtlessly into the very jaws of danger . . . the moment they step from the shop into the street."[18]

Reporting from Pittsburgh in 1907, Crystal Eastman wrote that "most of the men in the community whose opinions count . . . believe that 95 percent of the accidents are due to carelessnesss of the men"[19] (which is still the prevailing managerial view seven decades later).

Eastman disagreed with the practice of blaming the accident victims. She attributed accidents to "the speed and intensity of the work, the heat and the noise of the place, the weariness of the workers." In particular she singled out the worker's tendency to hurry that placed economic motives over safe practice: "in piecework, [hurrying] is encouraged by the worker's direct financial interest in the output. Oftener [sic] it is intensified by the pressure and speed at which the whole plant is run, an expression of the employer's direct financial interest in the output."[20]

Eastman cites examples of workers killed during their first night in the mill, whose deaths were attributed to inexperience, and of boys killed by ladles of molten iron while asleep at 1:30 A.M. because of fatigue. In fact, these accidents were among those that could have been prevented but for the following conditions:

1. Lack of provision of safety in construction
2. Long hours of work
3. Too great speed maintained in many lines
4. Inadequate plant inspection

5. Failure to remedy known defects
6. Inadequate warning and signal systems
7. Inadequate instruction and direction of ignorant workers[21]

In many instances injury was blamed on workers' violation of published work rules, but it has been suggested that rules were often published to satisfy legal requirements, while in practice, strict observance of safety rules was not permitted because it interfered with productivity goals. In the case of railroaders, for example, the official rules disseminated enjoined "great care in coupling and uncoupling cars. In all cases sufficient time must be taken to avoid accident or personal injury." This window dressing can be dramatically compared with a letter from management to the very workers supposedly covered by that rule. "Entirely too much time is being lost, especially on local trains, due to train and enginemen not taking advantage of conditions to gain time in doing their work, switching and unloading and loading of freight. Neither must you wait until train stops to get men into position."[22] The memorandum also stated that strict implementation of the safety rules on the railroad would have the same effect as a general strike, and those who adhered too closely to the officially decreed standard were threatened with dismissal.

In the textile industry, the extent of mechanization was cited as a source of injury. One industrial engineer cites figures that showed cotton mills to be equipped with 357 machines per 100 employees compared with 40 in furniture factories, 60 in rubber plants, and 67 in printing shops. He concluded that the greater the mechanical exposure, the greater the risk of injury. "The average cotton mill in Massachusetts has nearly a thousand employees and several thousand machines. The machines are usually belt driven. . . . Most of them have gears at several points on the machine. . . . The exposure points quickly run into the thousands or tens of thousands for a single plant."[23]

Frederick L. Hoffman drew a comparison between the level of occupational safety in the United States and in other countries, suggesting that accidents were more common here than abroad "partly because of the higher pressure under which our work is carried on and partly because of the rapid introduction of a new element of labor unfamiliar with our methods of mechanical production, but largely because of our general attitude of indifference toward human life itself."[24]

Despite the differences thus referred to, a great deal of testimony illuminating the problems of industrial safety has been developed abroad, especially in Great Britain. Testifying before a parliamentary committee in 1909, a senior lady inspector of factories attributed high accident rates in part to fatigue resulting from uninterrupted work of several hours' duration, overtime worked in combination with machinery, and the dangerous machinery used in piecework. Her most telling observation dealt with the experience of textile workers:

In weaving there is a good deal of driving. The weavers' earnings are taken round and shown to other weavers and put up in the shed and underlined, and the worker is made to be ashamed and very often works beyond her strength, or a tackler tries to screw weavers up to a certain amount of work, and that is done by a constant system of bullying. . . . That is a constant source of complaints and it is spoken of generally as increasing the risk of accidents.[25]

The committee concluded that accelerating the machines, increasing the amount of piecework demanded, and "driving" by employers led to increased injuries. In addressing carelessness, the committee asserted: "There is a large class of accidents sometimes said to be due to carelessness, but often arising from the inevitable fallibility of the human machine. . . . Such accidents are to be expected, especially when workers are constantly engaged at one monotonous operation, and the ultimate deadening of the faculty of attention leads to the brain failing to cooperate with the hand or foot."[26] Another witness before the same committee testified that "perhaps the reason why there were fewer laundry accidents in Scotland [than in England] was that there was less piecework."[27] Casual trades, such as dock work and construction labor, were also singled out as particularly hazardous; by nature they had a high labor turnover, and inexperience, as well as the frequently desperate plight of irregularly employed workers, was often exacerbated by unsafe practices.

Witness testimony by another deputy chief inspector attributed the lower accident rates in Scottish textile mills compared with English ones "to the fact that there is nothing like the same driving and the same rush to work there."[28] Another witness explained what was meant by rushing tactics, namely, that "work-people are not given sufficient time in which to perform their duties; and in their hurry often meet with accidents which they otherwise would not do."[29]

Though the testimony of British observers illuminates industrial conditions during this period, particularly the underlying causes of work injuries, factory inspection in Great Britain in 1909 was more effective than in the United States. Some observations on the level of factory inspection in Massachusetts will reveal the kind of attention the safety and health of factory workers received from state government.

A Fall River physician, testifying in 1910 before a commission investigating factory inspection in Massachusetts, indicated the thoroughness of these inspections.

Some inspectors go into the lower door of a factory on one side and come out on the other, and do it in a very short time, and record that as a factory inspection. I do not feel that is a factory inspection, I feel that is something of a farce. . . . the weaver room, if it is a reasonably large room, would take an inspector an entire day. . . . A man might put in his annual report that he has paid 400 visits to 220 factories. That is about the way these inspections are made. No man can do that and do it properly.[30]

Despite the impossibility of "doing it properly," factory inspectors did indeed record two to three inspections per day when each one, if done thoroughly, would have taken one or more days. The number of factory inspectors and the average yearly number of inspections in Massachusetts is given in Table 2.

TABLE 2. *Annual Factory Inspections in Massachusetts per Inspector, 1905 – 1908*

Year	Number of Inspectors	Average Yearly Number of Inspections per Inspector	Total Inspections
1905	14	715	10,008
1906	14	664	9,291
1907	15	643	9,683
1908	14	632	8,845

SOURCE: *Woman and Child Wage Earners in the United States*, Vol. 19 (Washington, D.C.: Government Printing Office, 1910), p. 34.

The duties of the inspectors were broad. Though the law authorized them to assess penalties in cases where management permitted machines to be cleaned while in operation, the chief inspector held the opinion that "the force of inspectors was too small to give attention to such detail,"[31] notwithstanding the fact that this was a major source of injury. Another duty was to determine the age of child operatives. The standard procedure was to ask young employees to complete a questionnaire. The response to these questionnaires is not surprising. "In no case did a child signing such a slip report itself as under 14 years of age. These age reports were not verified."[32]

Not only was the time insufficient for the number of inspections claimed, there was a shortage of inspectors. They would have had to inflate the numbers claimed in order to cover each establishment subject to at least annual inspection. That would have taken the existing inspection force into sixteen places per day. In addition to the criticisms of the perfunctory performance of the inspections, the practice of making political appointments to the inspectorate was deplored on the grounds that using these positions as spoils to reward the Grand Army of the Republic was counterproductive: "I do not think that it is absolutely necessary that the factory inspection force should be made up of men who are veterans of a war that was fought forty-six years ago," men who would inevitably be too old to perform adequately even if sufficient time were available.[33]

Finally, even if a sufficient number of competent and conscientious inspectors had been available, they probably would have been hindered by employer opposition to the performance of thorough inspections. Commenting on the situation in Pennsylvania around 1910, Florence Kelley noted: "Faithful inspectors insistent that the law should be obeyed, may be removed at will in the interests of powerful employers. This places a premium upon making friends with powerful interests, winking at violations of law, avoiding prosecution, publicity and everything that might provoke hostility."[34]

The 1910 Boston hearings dealt with another important facet of the struggle over health and safety. The chairman of the commission cited a provision of the law under which the state factory inspector could order the installation of exhaust fans in order to reduce dust, if they could be provided "without unreasonable expense."[35] This led to some discussion over who would decide what constituted an unreasonable expense. One of the members of the panel, a union official, was in favor of eliminating a potential danger to the worker: "No matter what the expense may be, if it is a menace to health it ought to be changed." The chairman argued that it was up to the inspectorate to determine whether an expense was unreasonable. To this the witness testified, "I think we had instructions from the [state] office not to give orders to entail undue expense."[36] Of course, then as now, cost was the sticking point, the focus of the conflict.

High casualty rates existed for non-English-speaking workers during this period, one in which millions of recent immigrants passed through the factory gates. Non-English speakers had a greater frequency of injuries than English speakers, an occurrence that may be attributed to two factors: (1) their inability to understand supervisory instructions given in a language foreign to them; and (2) the personnel practice of assigning the most recent immigrants to the worst jobs. An incident in coal mining around 1910 dramatizes the language problem: "An inspector . . . tells an immigrant miner, in English of course, that his roof needs propping. The miner seems to understand, but does not, and a fall results."[37] The ensuing fatality was then attributed to the ignorance and carelessness of the greenhorn.

The practice of placing immigrants in certain high-risk jobs was done, in part, out of necessity, since only the hungriest, most desperate applicants would submit to the conditions in some of these jobs. It was also a result of the employers' contempt for the immigrant, as illustrated by one of Alice Hamilton's experiences during a 1913 visit to a Utah lead-mining area: "When I asked an apothecary about lead poisoning in the neighborhood of the smelter, he said he had never known a case. I exclaimed that that was incredible and he said: 'Oh, maybe you are thinking of the Wops and Hunkies. I guess there's plenty among them. I thought you meant white men.'"[38] Hamilton observed that many employers hired immigrant labor "because it was cheap and submissive," but then they "washed their hands of all responsibility for accidents and sickness . . . because, as they would say, 'What can you do with a lot of ignorant Dagoes, Wops, Hunkies, Greasers?'"[39]

Effective union organization, which could have served to abate some of the adverse working conditions, was virtually nonexistent in the New England cotton mills during this period. According to a government document reporting a survey of the textile industry: "In New Bedford, Lowell and Manchester there are no union agreements and where any labor organizations exist they are very weak."[40] The only exception to this was Fall River, where a number of textile unions were able to survive. Copeland, writing in 1912, observed that among immigrants, who were predominant in the cotton mills, absence of union support

. . . has not been evidenced to the same degree by all nationalities. The English are usually the strongest union men, and the greater frequency of strikes in Fall River has been attributed, probably with justice, to the larger number of English employed there. Accustomed to unions in the "mother country," and more intelligent than many other immigrants, they have been ready to join hands in the common cause.[41]

The common cause was, in any case, confined mainly to negotiation of wage rates, for there is no evidence that health and safety conditions were better in Fall River than in the other textile centers.

The difference in union affiliation among the diverse ethnic groups in the cotton mills was documented in the survey *Immigrants in Industries*, which was based on a sample of 1,693 male employees. Among native white Americans, 10.5 percent were union members; among native-born of foreign fathers, 12.3 percent. Of the foreign born, union affiliation among the nationalities broke down as follows: English, 25.2 percent; Irish, 12.9 percent; Southern Italian, 12 percent; French Canadian, 10 percent; Portuguese, 2.7 percent; and Greek, 1.1 percent.[42]

There were many reasons for the low level of participation, including employer hostility toward unions to the extent that union activity jeopardized employment opportunities. Moreover, union officials demonstrated animosity toward recent immigrants who acquiesced in low wage rates and bad working conditions. Another factor affecting union participation was the agricultural background of many immigrant workers, who had little previous experience with unions and limited understanding upon first encountering factory organization.[43] With the exception of the English-born mill workers, the majority of the immigrant cotton mill operatives were former peasants or farm laborers.

Among the English immigrants in *Immigrants in Industry*, 70.4 percent of the men and 94.2 percent of the women had worked in textile factories in Great Britain before coming to the United States, and their previous experience undoubtedly facilitated their adaptation to the technology and social organization of the American factory. Along with the Irish im-

TABLE 3. *Percentage of Immigrant Cotton Mill Operatives with Agricultural Background*

Nationality	Total Males	Male Peasants or Farm Laborers		Total Females	Female Peasants or Farm Laborers	
		Number	Percent		Number	Percent
English	2,082	21	1.0	1,136	—	—
French Canadian	3,191	2,100	65.8	726	336	46.3
Polish	3,862	3,191	82.6	2,488	2,246	90.3
Portuguese	2,379	1,684	70.8	388	82	21.1
Greek	1,498	892	59.5	92	56	60.9
Irish	1,260	549	43.6	391	40	10.2

SOURCE: *Immigrants in Industries* (Washington, D.C.: Government Printing Office, 1910), pp. 363–64.

migrants they were also spared a disability of many others, namely, inability to understand the language spoken by the management. Among the foreign-born mill operatives there was a high proportion of non-English speakers.

The language problem figured significantly in matters of health and safety. It also affected union organization because ethnic hostilities served to undermine solidarity among mill employees. A case from the Dwight Manufacturing Company illustrates this kind of hostility. Polish loom fixers objected to a Greek weaver being upgraded into their classification. The Polish workers asked the supervisor to discharge the Greek, whose initiation fee was refused by the loom fixers' union as a result of the Poles' antagonism. The mill agent complained in a letter to the United Textile Workers president: "[I] have known that the Polish people did not like the Greek people coming here, but have thought this to be unfair, inasmuch as there was no opposition to the Polish people coming here when the French were in the majority."[44]

A mill staffed like the construction gang on the Tower of Babel conferred an advantage on the managers. The effect of ethnic disharmony should not be exaggerated in comparison with the effects of employer hostility toward unions. According to the study on women and child wage earners, mill officials in only 3 of 46 New England cotton mills (6.5 percent) de-

TABLE 4. *English-Speaking Ability of Immigrant Cotton Mill Operatives*

Nationality	Percentage Unable to Speak English	
	Male	Female
French Canadian	24.4	45.8
Portuguese	55.3	73.1
Polish	74.1	92.5
Greek	74.1	93.1

SOURCE: *Immigrants in Industries*, pt. 3, p. 209.

scribed themselves as "approving of unions" while 21 (45.6 percent) were "opposed to unions," with the remainder reported as indifferent or noncommittal.[45]

The trials of cotton mill employment were compounded for the women operatives by a number of factors. Few women belonged to unions. The secretary of the Boston Central Labor Union indicated just how welcome they were when he wrote in 1897 that the "invasion of the crafts by women has been developing for years amid irritation and injury to the workman. . . . The growing demand for female labor . . . is an insidious assault upon the home. . . . and very soon the shop or factory are [sic] full of women, while their fathers have the option of working for the same wages or a few cents more, or to take their place in the large army of unemployed."[46]

Not only craft union mentality but also patriarchal family relationships served to isolate women from wider social contacts, as witnessed by the markedly greater proportion in several ethnic groups of women than men who were unable to speak English. This was reflected not only in the absence of women from unions but in their reported attitudes toward labor organization. In a 1908 survey of women in cotton mills, among 543 women interviewed, 19.5 percent described themselves as being favorable toward unions; 10.7 percent as unfavorable; 13.3 percent as indifferent; while a majority, 56.5 percent said they had "no opinion because of ignorance on the subject."[47]

Even when well organized, unions seem to deal more effectively with wages, workloads, and factory discipline than with occupational hazards. In the early part of the twentieth century, the circumstances in the New England cotton mills with respect to unionization were far from optimal, and this lack of organization had detrimental effects on the workers' health and safety.

CONDITIONS IN FALL RIVER, MASSACHUSETTS

The status of cotton mill operatives compared with that of other segments of the population is nowhere better documented than in the vital statistics and health records for 1908 to 1912 in Fall River, Massachusetts, which was at that time the largest cotton manufacturing center in the United States. Information on mortality rates, earnings, housing conditions, and other variables has been preserved, and it illuminates the class inequalities under which the cotton operatives labored.

A major mortality survey in which a physician investigated the deaths in Fall River of 1,983 persons between the ages of 15 and 44 during 1908–12 revealed that cotton mill operatives were "on the average one and one-half times as liable to die as nonoperatives of practically identical age."[48] The key factor that accounted for this differential was the greater susceptibility of mill workers to tuberculosis because of their unsanitary work environment and substandard housing.

To those of us living in a time and place who take for granted a clean drink of water on the job, the problems attendant upon this simple need in the Fall River cotton mills around 1910 must seem incredible. Yet at hearings in that year on the inspection of factories, testimony was given indicating that city water was unavailable in many textile plants except in the mill yard. The lack of running water on the upper floors was, according to Fall River health officer Dr. MacKnight, "because it is an expensive operation for the mill. If they provide drinking water, the law does not say where it shall be provided."[49] In the place of running water, workers relied on a barrel of water and a common cup. Dr. MacKnight was questioned about the legality of this practice: "Do I understand that the mills are exempt from this new law that requires the disuse of the public drinking cup?" His reply was yes.[50]

In addition to the hazard embodied by the public cup, the condition of the water barrels into which these cups were dipped left a lot to be desired. Not only were they repositories of the air-borne cotton fibers, dust, and dried sputum that contaminated the atmosphere, but according to MacKnight:

> The man who carries the water is the man who scrubs the water closets, and a great many times he scrubs out the water closet before he cleans the barrel, and often with the same mop. That has been proven more than once. . . . A great many times the mops after they have been used to clean out the water closet are set mop end up and drip into the barrel. . . . The ice carried to the top floor is sometimes carried in the same pail that is used to clean the water closets.[51]

The ice referred to had to be paid for by a "voluntary" subscription of the employees that was collected by a supervisor, but no guarantees of its purity were given.

Not only were hazards to health and safety countenanced by the mill management, but employee complaints were discouraged. Dr. MacKnight testified that five to ten workers visited his office nightly to report about adverse mill conditions, and labor unions sent reports as well, but under the law complaints had to be in writing and signed by the worker.[52] This eliminated complaints for two reasons: first, mill workers were "unwilling to put their signatures to anything for fear of discharge," and second, many mill workers had difficulty expressing themselves in writing.[53]

The general impact of working conditions on life expectancy was documented by the positive correlation between length of service and mortality rates. Though the pattern was not consistent, in a U.S. Department of Labor report of 1919, Arthur Perry concluded that "among cotton-mill operatives of similar age the factor of mill work as a contributory cause of death is active commonly according to the length of the period of employment in the mill."[54] The hazards derived from conditions in the mill were compounded by the standard of living to which the prevailing wage rates subjected the mill operatives and their families. This is nowhere better documented than in the data on housing conditions.

Investigation into workers' housing included on-site assessment of hygiene, along with collection of information on the number of occupants per room and the rental cost. Accessibility of sunlight, location and condition of toilets, and crowding were taken into account.

Among cotton operatives aged 15–44 who died during the period of 1908–12, the proportion who had lived in hygienically unsatisfactory dwellings was significantly greater than among nonoperatives, both in deaths from tuberculosis and from nontuberculous causes.[55] Within each occupational division, moreover, the victims of tuberculosis had occupied poorer housing than those who had died from all other causes.

The amount of rent per capita per year was another indicator of the standard of housing at that time. Cotton mill operatives occupied cheaper housing than nonoperatives, and within each group tuberculous decedents had lived in dwellings with lower average rent than nontuberculous decedents (see Table 5).

With respect to crowding, cotton operatives lived in more densely occupied housing than nonoperatives, and within each occupational category the tuberculosis victims came from more crowded dwellings than those who had died from other causes. For all causes of death, operatives came from dwellings with 22 percent more occupancy per room than nonoperatives (see Table 6).

TABLE 5. *Average Per Capita Yearly Rent of Decedents, 1905–1907*

	Tuberculous	Nontuberculous
Operatives	$17.63	$20.64
Nonoperatives	22.41	27.46

SOURCE: Perry, *Preventable Death in Cotton Manufacturing Industry*, U.S. Department of Labor, Bureau of Labor Statistics Bulletin No. 251 (Washington, D.C.: Government Printing Office, 1919), p. 373.

TABLE 6. *Average Persons Per Room in Homes of Decedents, 1905–1907*

	Tuberculous	Nontuberculous
Operatives	1.21	1.06
Nonoperatives	1.03	.89

SOURCE: Perry, *Preventable Death*, p. 369.

Though Dr. Perry's survey took him into the home of every decedent from 1908 to 1912, during his two years of field work in Fall River, the tabulation of his findings does not evoke fully the squalor in which the most poorly housed decedents had lived. For a more graphic image of just what it meant to live in unhygienic dwellings in the cotton capital during this period it is necessary to turn to a report commissioned in December 1911 by the Associated Charities of Fall River. The investigation inspected a sample of the most unsanitary tenements in the city in order to make a case for housing improvements. The agency appointed for this task inspected 1,171 apartments in 279 buildings that housed 5,980 persons (about 5 percent of the city's population) comprising 4,961 members of families and 537 lodgers.

In certain instances kitchens served also as sleeping rooms (in 30 cases of 1171), which resulted in the following horrendous circumstances:

In five such cases lodgers were found to be occupants of the kitchen beds, one of whom was unquestionably in the last stages of tuberculosis. The family dog and the children were using the same kitchen as a playroom. That the family pet was carrying the disease to the children and the adults of the family was evident from that fact that at the time of the investigating agent's call the dog partook of the contents of the open cuspidor.[56]

The survey's 1912 findings of only 32 bathtubs in 1,171 apartments (2.7 percent) indicate the low priority landlords placed on the personal hygiene of poor tenants. In addition, the investigating agents found 64 of the 279 dwelling structures

(22.9 percent) to be of questionable fitness for human habitation because of leaking roofs, broken doors, and dangerous stairways.[57] Wooden fire escapes or fire escapes with metal railings and wooden platforms were found in 101 buildings (36.2 percent), and there were two buildings without fire escapes.[58] In regards to crowding, the ratio of occupants per room exceeded the averages of the mortality survey cited above, with 1.3 persons per room in apartments without lodgers and 1.7 per room in apartments shared with lodgers.[59]

Toilets for the 5,980 Fall River residents in the housing surveyed were often inadequate. Of the 1,171 apartments, 659 (56.3 percent) had their own toilets, while the remaining 239 toilets were shared by two or more residential units. The shared toilets—located in halls, cellars, and yards—were described as particularly unsanitary (see Table 7).

The kitchen location of many toilets was attributed to the need to keep the pipes from freezing in the winter, and often the kitchen was the only room that could be heated. In such cases, proper lighting and ventilation was often impossible, so that 76 of 117 totally unventilated toilets (65 percent) were kitchen toilets. In 16 kitchen toilets the partitions separating the toilet from the rest of the kitchen did not reach the ceiling.

Sanitary conditions of cellar or basement toilets were even worse, especially in winter, when water had to be shut off to

TABLE 7. *Toilet Facilities in Fall River Tenements, 1911*

Location	Number	Percentage	Percentage Dirty or Filthy	Percentage Poorly or Not Ventilated
Hall	88	9.9	46.6	56.8
Pantry	71	7.9	23.9	36.6
Kitchen	389	43.3	42.2	50.9
Cellar or Basement	298	33.1	54.7	56.4
Other	52	5.8	48.1	51.9
TOTAL	898	100.0	46.4	47.8

SOURCE: Carol Aronovici, *Housing Conditions in Fall River* ([Fall River, Mass.]: Associated Charities Housing Committee, n.d.), p. 12.

prevent freezing. In cases where water was not shut off, toilets froze and the inspectors found human feces on the floor.[60]

"Tuberculosis," wrote Alice Hamilton in 1906, "is a disease of the working classes," and in a later commentary referred to this disease as "perhaps the first penalty society had to pay for the capitalistic exploitation of labor."[61] In every age group the mortality from tuberculosis was significantly higher among mill operatives than among the remainder of the population.

In the hot, humid and ill-ventilated mill rooms, in air laden with cotton dust, the tubercle bacillus emitted by coughing and spitting found a hospitable environment and numerous new victims to infect. Unsanitary working conditions were compounded by low wages, fatigue, excessive exertion, and insufficient rest as a result of long work shifts.[62] Associated with low wages were poor nutrition, inadequate housing, and pressure to send children into the mill to augment the family income. Exhausting labor and insufficient sleep also lowered the body's resistance to the ravages of disease. The working and living conditions of tuberculous mill hands were the very antithesis of the sanatorium.

This situation was exacerbated in the case of married women whose potential rest time was diminished by an average of 2.8 hours per day of housework upon completion of their shift in the mill.[63]

Furthermore, in an age when contraception was still in minimal use, especially among the working class, frequent births and postpartum stress, complicated by tuberculosis, increased mortality. At that time the majority was under religious constraint against abortion to save a tuberculous mother.

The tuberculosis death rate was 5.56 per 1000 among the married women mill workers compared with 2.09 per 1000 among the unmarried, while among those not employed in the mills the rate was 1.42 per 1000 among the married women and 1.36 per 1000 among the unmarried.[64] The relationship between tuberculosis deaths and conjugal conditions was reversed among males, the unmarried among both mill workers and non-mill workers experiencing a higher death rate than the married.

Knowledge that tuberculosis is caused by bacteria dates from the 1880s, and the requirement in Massachusetts to report cases of this contagious disease dates from 1907. Nevertheless, according to the previously cited medical witness, Dr. Mac-Knight, mill managers apparently were indifferent to the spread of infection among their operatives. His testimony from hearings in 1910 reveals the lack of concern over tuberculous mill workers:

> Q. We have heard that there are a good many tubercular sub-
>   jects . . . in the cotton mills. If you find such subjects . . .
>   are they taken out of the mills?
> A. Not the adults.
> Q. Don't the mill superintendents get rid of them?
> A. No.
> Q. Of course you have the right to take out minors and
>   women?
> A. No, we have not any right at all.[65]

Among the sources of infection in the mills, one in particular contributed to the hazards faced by weavers, namely, the shuttle that operatives threaded by oral suction. Another physician from Fall River, Dr. J. W. Coughlin, testified:

> If there be in this whole State an instrument of greater destruction I
> do not know it. . . . I believe that no human lips can touch that wood
> that has become infected by the virus of tuberculosis without im-
> parting it to the lips of a virgin constitution and ultimately impreg-
> nating that constitution and destroying that life; . . . what must the
> danger be in that, where the weaver, wavering and tottering at her
> looms, whose life is almost on the verge of extinguishment, who
> goes home and dies of tuberculosis and an innocent operative comes
> and sucks that shuttle to which her mouth or his mouth has been
> placed for months prior to the death of that previous operative.[66]

If the mill management was not averse to keeping tuber-culous employees on the job, the disease as it progressed eventually disabled them to the extent that they could no longer perform their duties and thereafter remained either at home or in a hospital. Conditions in the hospital were subjected to critical scrutiny during this period. "As a result of complaints made to the Fall River Medical Society as to conditions at the consumptive shacks at the City hospital, a committee of three physicians . . . made an investigation and found matters even worse than reported to them. During the recent severe storm patients' beds were soaked and the floor of the shacks covered with water, and patients were without attendance for 12 hours."[67]

In November 1910 a new contagious disease hospital was put into use for tuberculosis patients, in which an average of 53 patients per day were cared for during 1911 at an average cost of $4.00 per patient per week. The occupational classification of tuberculosis patients in this hospital was published in the Board of Health Reports for 1911.[68]

The per capita weekly income in the families of male tuberculosis victims also supports the designation of tuberculosis as a disease of the poor. Income data for 1911 and 1912 decedents (aged 15–44 in families of two or more members) showed no significant difference between cotton operatives and nonoperatives with regards to income, with 66.7 percent of the former and 61.0 percent of the latter below $5 per capita per week.[69] The nonoperative population had a significantly lower mortality rate from tuberculosis than the operatives, but those among the nonoperatives who died from it were just about as poor as the cotton mill victims. In contrast to the dead from tuberculosis, among the nontuberculous decedents those who were not cotton mill operatives had significantly higher per capita family income, among nonoperatives 59.4 percent with $5 or more per capita per week and operatives 41.7 percent.[70]

The death rate from tuberculosis of cotton operatives exceeded by 113 percent the rate for nonoperatives in the 15–24 age range, by 77 percent in the 25–34 age range, and by 112 percent in the 35–44 range. For women operatives the excess mortality in comparison with nonoperatives was much greater than among men: 134 percent, 144 percent, and 154 percent for women in the three age brackets, compared with 60 percent, 23 percent, and 76 percent for men. As in a number of other categories, compared with nonoperatives of each sex, the "deficit" in the life chances of women operatives was greater than that of men. The explanation for this difference lies in the fact that 66.8 percent of gainfully employed women in Fall River were in the cotton mills compared with 29.4 percent of the employed men. A large proportion of male nonoperative decedents were exposed to the hazards of other occupations, while a large proportion of the female population (58 percent of those aged 10 or over in 1910 compared with 17 percent of the same-aged males) was not employed outside the home. Female labor force participation in Fall River at that time generally took place in families as a result of the pressure of insufficient earning of the men.

Deaths in which pregnancy-related factors constituted the principal or contributory cause were frequent occurrences in the years from 1908 to 1912. In Fall River, the maternal mortality rates of married cotton mill operatives in the principal child-bearing age brackets were far greater than among nonoperatives of corresponding ages.[71] Among cotton mill operatives aged 15 to 24, the maternal death rate was 4.72 per 1,000 married women, compared with .64 per 1,000 among nonoperatives; while in the 25 to 34 age bracket maternal deaths were 4.68 per 1,000 among women mill workers and 1.69 among the nonoperatives.

In discussing the inequalities of class it would be difficult to single out a factor more germane to differential life chances than the disparity in the probability of surviving to one's first birthday. The infant mortality rate among children born to cotton mill operatives compared with the rate among children of nonoperatives exemplifies the distinction between these two classes and is central to the present topic.

While the Perry study provides data only for decedent mothers who were predeceased by children and thus does not yield a true infant mortality rate, it does dramatically document the differences between cotton operatives' families and those of nonoperatives. Similarly, Dublin found that of 802 live births in Fall River during June, July, and August 1913, those whose mothers were gainfully employed (almost entirely mill workers) had an infant mortality rate nearly double those born to mothers who were housewives. In the same study, fathers differentiated by occupation yielded an infant mortality rate of 201.8 per 1000 births among the babies whose fathers were in textile occupations and 184.7 for all other occupations.[72]

The Fall River record validates Arnold Toynbee's trenchant observation that "free competition could create wealth without creating well-being."[73] The differences in mortality rates of cotton mill operatives and nonoperatives greatly understate class inequalities because a majority of nonoperatives were also wage laborers or their dependents. However, the priority of textiles in early industrialization and the position of Fall River as the largest cotton manufacturing city in the United States at that time underscore the cost in suffering exacted by this industry.

THE LAW OF THE KILLED AND WOUNDED

In a 1906 article William Hard asked the perhaps rhetorical question why society does not, "having invented machines which make business one long war, treat the enlisted men at least like enlisted men and, if they are incapacitated, assign them temporarily or permanently, to the rank and pay of pensioners of peace?"[74] The answer to his question was that changes in the laws that governed the treatment of industrial casualties lagged behind other changes in technology and in social relationships that accompanied the industrial revolution.[75]

The law is not a set of impartial norms based on immutable truths, but a codification of rules based on the relationships of power in society. It is, in the words of Brooks Adams, "established by the dominant class, so far as it can impose its will upon those who are weaker." This holds true for statute law, in which the social background of the legislators and the pressures of various constituencies shape the course of legislation. It is even more applicable, as will be seen below, in the realm of judge-made common law. Economic production, Harold Laski pointed out, depends on domestic peace, and he went on to say that "the state must maintain law and order to that end. But in so doing, it is necessarily maintaining the law and order implied in the particular system of class-relations of which it is the expression."[76] Thus the inference can be drawn that at the time Hard raised his question, the social forces that sought reform of the law on occupational hazards had not gathered enough strength to secure for industrial casualties the sort of compensation that had been established for military casualties.

Payment of compensation to victims of injury or to their kin is a practice of great antiquity.[77] Instituted as a social control mechanism to abate feuds, such payments were designed to "make better" if not to "make whole," the injured parties at the expense of those who wronged them. The laws of Ethelbert, King of Kent, dating from the first decade of the seventh century, specified payment by the guilty party for injuries in the amount of fifty shillings for an eye, twelve for an ear, twenty for a thumb, nine for a forefinger, six for a tooth, and one for a fingernail.[78]

Thirteen centuries later, the 1911 Massachusetts law "relative to the payments to employees for personal injuries received in the course of their employment" stipulated the following dismemberment schedule:

(a) For the loss by severance of both hands at or above the wrist, or both feet at or above the ankle, or the loss of one hand and one foot, or the entire and irrevocable loss of the sight of both eyes, one half of the average weekly wages of the injured person, but not more than ten dollars nor less than four dollars a week, for a period of one hundred weeks.
(b) For the loss by severance of either hand at or above the wrist, or either foot at or above the ankle, or the entire and irrevocable loss of the sight of either eye, one half the average weekly wages of

the injured person, but not more than ten dollars nor less than four dollars a week, for a period of fifty weeks.

(c) For the loss by severance at or above the second joint of two or more fingers, including thumbs, or toes, one half of the average weekly wages of the injured person, but not more than ten dollars nor less than four dollars a week, for a period of twenty-five weeks.

(d) For the loss by severance of at least one phalange of a finger, thumb or toe, one half the average weekly wages of the injured person, but not more than ten dollars nor less than four dollars a week, for a period of twelve weeks.[79]

The differences between these two dismemberment schedules should be emphasized. The seventh-century version was predicated on establishment of guilt for a criminal act, while the twentieth-century schedule marked the emergence of social insurances as a basis for recompense in cases of injuries suffered by workers in the course of their employment. The workmen's compensation laws provided for payments in such cases without assessment of fault. These laws superseded a dispensation under tort law in which a clear-cut determination of fault was necessary.

Payment of reparations reflected, from early times down to the present, the rank in society, because the wergild payable under Anglo-Saxon law for the death of a king or nobleman was greater than that paid for the death of a commoner or slave. By the same token the death benefits and injury compensation under the 1911 Massachusetts law were tied to the weekly wage rate of the victim. When contractual employment replaced servile labor, injured employees began to have recourse to the common law of torts, under which they could recover damages if they were successful in litigation that established the employer's negligence as the proximate cause of injury. It was the business of tort law, according to Justice Holmes, "to fix the dividing lines between those cases in which a man is liable for harm which he has done, and those in which he is not."[80] The class of industrial tort-feasors had an interest in drawing these lines as narrowly as possible, and the common law courts obliged them by creating for injured servants often insurmountable obstacles to recovery in litigation against their masters.

Under the common law it was the duty of employers to take reasonable care to provide a safe workplace, proper instruction regarding hazards, an adequate number of competent fellow servants, and a set of work rules.[81] These obligations were hedged by numerous restrictions and were virtually nullified by defenses used by the employers, such as contributory negligence, assumption of risk, and the fellow servant rule. Prosser labeled these the "unholy trinity" and the "three wicked sisters" of the common law.[82]

The most frequently invoked of the common law "wicked sisters" was the principle of contributory negligence under which a plaintiff was defeated in work injury litigation unless he could prove that at the time of his injury he had been exercising due care and diligence. Contributory negligence is "any want of ordinary care on the part of the person injured . . . which . . . contributed to the injury as a proximate cause thereof, and as an element without which the injury could not have occurred."[83] As revealed by the injury reports examined in this study, the employer's agents attributed carelessness to the victim almost as a matter of course.

Yet, carelessness was an issue. Roscoe Pound pointed out that "the supposed contributory negligence of employees is in effect a result of the mechanical conditions imposed on them by the nature of their employment, and . . . by reason of these conditions the individual vigilance and responsibility contemplated by the common law is impossible in practice." A later commentary referred to this common law principle as "a Draconian rule sired by a medieval concept of cause out of a heartless laissez-faire."[84]

Crystal Eastman argued that the notion of contributory negligence was defined on the basis of what an ordinary prudent man would do in a situation, but that it was "practically impossible to apply such a test justly to workmen engaged in hazardous occupations." It was a legal provision that was biased against the worker who had to prove not only that the employer was negligent but also to exculpate himself. In the ordinary case he had to do this despite great difficulty in securing witnesses because there were no constraints against employers' dismissal of workers who testified on behalf of a plaintiff in an injury case.[85]

At the Lincoln Summer Assizes in England in 1836, a butcher's boy named Priestly won a judgment against his employer of £100 for a broken thigh bone suffered in the collapse of a wagon overloaded with mutton and beef. On appeal, the judges headed by Lord Abinger invented the fellow-servant rule when they reversed this decision on the grounds that it was "'inconvenient' and 'absurd' for masters to be responsible for the negligence of their servants," the wagon having been overloaded not by the defendant Fowler, but by another of his employees. Based on a doctrine that Parry called "largely a figment of the judicial imagination," this decision "set back . . . the hour of industrial reform for more than one generation." Parry was unequivocal in identifying the class bias embodied by the decision:

No doubt the judges of 1836, being men connected with the upper middle classes of the day, could not conceive how civilisation and social order could exist side by side with a wicked system whereby a master had to compensate a workman injured in his service. The thing was as incomprehensible to the judicial mind of that date as the fifth proposition of Euclid is to many a third-form schoolboy of today. Some of our judges are still in the third form in their ideas of sociology. That is one of the dangers of judge-made law. It is bound to put the stamp of old-fashioned class prejudice on its judges. If the judges had been labour leaders they would have discovered an implied contract for the master to pay compensation with equal complacency.[86]

This English judicial invention was imported into the United States with all deliberate speed. A locomotive engineer named Farwell suffered a serious injury as the result of a derailment attributed to the negligence of a switchman. His damage suit against the Boston and Worcester Railroad was defeated in a famous 1842 decision by Chief Justice Lemuel Shaw, who ruled that "the implied contract of the master does not extend to indemnify the servant against the negligence of anyone but himself; and he is not liable in tort, as for the negligence of his servant."[87] This reasoning has been widely construed as an abrogation of the principle of *respondeat superior*, which holds the master liable for injuries caused by a subordinate. If the switchman had been an employee of another railroad, or if Farwell had been a passenger or other "stranger," he would have won damages in the case. This decision relieved the entrepreneurial class "of an enormous financial burden for industrial accidents which it would otherwise have incurred." According to Chief Justice Shaw considerations of "justice" required an employee to take upon himself "the natural and ordinary risks and perils" inherent in the position, including "perils arising from the negligence of fellow servants."[88] The fellow-servant rule is thus seen as one aspect of the principle of assumption of risk.

Applying the assumption of risk doctrine, the third of the common law "wicked sisters," did much, according to Labatt, "to embitter the feeling with which capitalists are regarded by the working classes."[89] It referred to those hazards "that are incidental to a relationship of free association . . . which either [party] is at liberty to take or leave as he will."[90] Because the worker presumably knew of the danger inherent in the job, he was not entitled to recover on injuries resulting from that danger. Theodore Roosevelt denounced this legal doctrine in relation to the case of Sarah Kniseley. Sarah Kniseley lost her arm in a defective machine, but the courts ruled in favor of the employer because the plaintiff had continued working on her job even though she knew of the defect. This principle rests on what the employee knew or should have known about ordinary or unusual hazards in the course of work:

An adult female employee, though she has just gone to work and is unfamiliar with machinery, is presumed to understand without instruction, the danger of getting her hands caught in the cogwheels on the machine she is operating (Ruchinsky v. French [1897] 168 Mass. 68, 46 N.E. 417). An employer may properly assume that even a boy of fourteen need not be told that, if he puts his fingers into gearing, they will be crushed (Silvia v. Sagamore Mfg. Co. [1901] 177 Mass. 476, 59 N.E. 73).[91]

Labatt argued that in effect assumption of risk was a type of contributory negligence, because a "master, in permitting his machinery to be more than ordinarily dangerous, is guilty of negligence, while the servant by remaining with full knowledge of the resulting risks, contributes to his own injury. The causal connection between the employer's negligence and the injury is said to be broken at the time that the danger becomes so plain that a person of ordinary care would not incur the risk of continuing to work at the place of danger."[92]

The employee's fear of losing his job because of refusing to work on a dangerous machine or to face other hazards was not admitted as evidence of constraint, even though some courts have admitted that this "furnishes protection to employers whose conduct may be described as immoral or inhuman."[93] The worker's freedom of choice was not impaired by fear of losing his job, and this freedom of a contractual relationship between supposedly equal parties was the premise on which the doctrine rested. To uphold it, according to Labatt, it was "necessary to accept the most extreme doctrine of the laissez-faire school of sociologists."[94] The court put a great deal of stress on the free will of the worker, even in cases where exercising that free will went against the workers' self-interest. Prosser wrote that "in the absence of statute the greater number of courts held that a risk is assumed even when a workman acts under a direct command carrying an express or implied threat of discharge for disobedience."[95]

This principle was "first announced in all its repulsive nakedness" by Lord Bramwell in a case in which "the appliance which caused the injury had been deliberately substituted for one of the safe type generally used, for no other reason than that it was less expensive."[96] According to the decision, "a master is entitled to carry on his business in a dangerous way 'if the servant is foolish enough to agree to it.'"[97]

It may be inhuman so to carry on his works as to expose his workmen to peril of their lives, but it does not create a right of action for an injury which it may occasion, when . . . the workman has known all the facts and is as well acquainted as the master with the nature of the machinery, and voluntarily uses it. . . . Morally speaking, those who employ men in dangerous work without doing all in their power to obviate the danger are highly reprehensible. . . . But looking at the matter in a legal point of view, if a man, for the sake of employment takes it or continues in it with a knowledge of its risks he must trust to himself to keep clear of injury.[98]

Labatt commented that to describe a worker who is driven by fear of unemployment as a "voluntary agent" is "a mere trifling with words."[99]

As in the case of *Priestly* v. *Fowler* and the fellow-servant rule, the views of the English law lords on the matter of assumption of risk created a sympathetic echo among American judges. In a railroad injury case Justice Bradley wrote in 1887 that any doctrine opposed to the assumption of risk "would subject employers to unreasonable and often ruinous responsibilities, thereby embarrassing all branches of business," as well as encouraging carelessness. In a later railroad case in 1943, Mr. Justice Black observed that this was "a judicially created rule which was developed in response to the general impulse of common law courts at the beginning of this period to insulate the employer as much as possible from bearing the 'human overhead' which is an inevitable cost—to someone—of the doing of industrialized business."[100]

Attempts to modify the common law dispensation came with the enactment of employers' liability statutes. Massachusetts passed such an act in 1887, the first in the United States. It perpetuated the three wicked sisters of the common law, but modified the fellow servant rule. The act excluded from its coverage negligence by such "vice principals" as su-

pervisory personnel and those employees who had "the duty of
seeing that the ways, works or machinery were in proper condition." In addition, the act established the maximums in the
amount of $5,000 for death benefits and of $4,000 for personal
injury awards.[101] Under this type of statute, litigation remained
the pathway to remedy, although insurance carriers routinely
avoided court cases by offering small settlements in exchange
for a signed release.

Weiss summarized the shortcomings of employers' liability
as a method for dealing with injuries: only a small proportion
of injured workers recovered substantial damages and many received nothing; there were long delays in the procedures; only
a small proportion of employers' liability insurance expenditures served the injury victims or their kin; and the antagonism between employers and employees was exacerbated.[102]

Under the liability laws, as Sutherland pointed out, each
party in the adversary proceedings had a motive for distorting
and misrepresenting the facts in order to prevail in court.[103]
Pinning blame on the opposing party in the suit and exculpat-
ing oneself, he suggested, intensified industrial conflict. In line
with this thinking, social insurance proponents argued that reform of the laws of occupational injury would be conducive to
greater harmony between employer and employee.

Employers' liability laws unduly favored employers, in Eastman's view, as evidenced by the rules for adjudicating work injuries. "The law is behindhand, and the law makers have been
blind. With their minds . . . steeped in old ideas of theoretical
equality and freedom of contract, they have gone on, content
with the 'logic of law,' oblivious to actual facts."[104]

Hard called the requirement of litigation under the employers' liability laws "a deep down vice." In effect, society tells the
steelworker who loses an arm:

"Go ahead and sue the U.S. Steel Corporation. The courts are open
to you just as they are open to the U.S. Steel Corporation. . . . You
are at liberty to try to starve out the U.S. Steel Corporation just as
the U.S. Steel Corporation is at liberty to try to starve you out." . . .

He and his wife are hungry, and the law says to him that in two and a half years he may possibly find out whether anything is coming to him or not. Litigation is a rich man's game, like automobiling and yachting.[105]

Notwithstanding the legal fiction of equality between litigants, delay invariably aided the more affluent party to the suit. Thus it was true that the "bedside settlement is generally the cheapest." As a further deterrent to litigation, the insurance companies insisted "upon the dismissal of any man who brings suit."[106]

In the adversary process spelled out under the employers' liability laws, the impoverished victims of industrial injuries had to rely on the services of attorneys practicing on a contingent fee basis. While these practitioners who thus served the poor "were denounced by the professional elite as inferior ambulance chasers or shysters,"[107] they provided virtually the only available legal representation that could be gotten by injured workers. A New York state study of 51 employers' liability awards recorded that lawyers' contingent fees in 41.1 percent of the cases amounted to 35 percent or more of the settlement; in 32.4 percent of the cases, fees were 25 to 34.9 percent of the settlement; and in the remaining 26.5 percent, fees were under 25 percent of the award.[108] "In this diabolical game a negligence lawyer could claim a sufficiently high percentage from his successful suits to compensate for his losses."[109]

"No fault" workmen's compensation laws, exemplified by the 1911 Massachusetts act and dismemberment schedule cited above, created a new set of ground rules for dealing with work injury cases, under which the specter of contributory negligence was laid to rest. Beginning with a federal employee's compensation statute in 1908 and ending in 1948 when Mississippi became the last state to adopt workmen's compensation laws, passage of such legislation has been among the important worker safety reforms and will be discussed further in chapter 5.

CHAPTER 3

Patterns of Contributory Negligence

O LIVA BOURQUE'S boyhood was shattered at the age of fourteen in the summer of 1896, when he lost his right arm in the mule spinning department of the Lyman Mills in Holyoke, Massachusetts. After six weeks on the job at a weekly wage of $4.60, young Bourque's arm was caught in a machine, necessitating amputation between the shoulder and elbow. The overseer's report stated that "the boy was careless. If he had done his work as he had been instructed he would not have been caught."[1] The liability insurer agreed to pay the hospital bill but expressed the judgment that "no legal liability existed and under all the circumstances perhaps no claim will be made."[2] On October 20, 1896, Oliva Bourque was paid one dollar, and a final payment (in exchange for a release signed by the victim and by his father) was made on December 12, 1896 in the amount of $31.20.

The employer's defense of the worker's contributory negligence—the most obtrusive of the common law "wicked sisters"—was used against Oliva Bourque and many of his fellow workers in a most painful way. Only an employee who was "himself in the exercise of due care and diligence," was entitled to damages in case of injury, and employers saved countless thousands of dollars by the expedient of blaming the victim.

This chapter deals with injuries and the employer practice of imputing contributory negligence at the Lyman Mills In Holyoke, Massachusetts during the period from 1895 to 1916. The data are derived from injury reports and correspondence between the mill management and the liability insurer.

The Lyman Mills complex during this period was a typical cotton cloth manufacturing facility consisting of four buildings that included carding, spinning, drawing and weaving rooms, a cloth room, and a shop and yard force serving the entire mill. During the pay period ending July 7, 1900 there were 1,291 employees at Lyman, a force consisting of 556 men and boys (43.1 percent) and 735 women and girls (56.9 percent).

Lyman case records reporting injuries to workers identify the physical agencies or events that were the immediate cause of injury.[3] Of 814 cases in which this information is available, 513 (63.0 percent) were a result of workers having a part of their bodies caught in moving machinery or elevators. Of the remaining 301 injuries (37.0 percent), 76 were caused by flying shuttles or falling objects, 68 by falls, 75 by wounds from metal or broken glass, 16 eye injuries, 12 burns, and 54 were categorized as miscellaneous.

The high proportion of injuries attributed to moving parts of machines, such as gears, pulleys, belts, beaters, circular saws, and other mechanical devices, demonstrates the low level of enforcement of the 1877 Massachusetts law requiring that machinery be equipped with covers to guard moving parts.[4] The extent of injury resulting from machinery reflects the hazards entailed by a technology relying on belts connected to shafting which in turn was geared to a central power source. Elevators lacked safe enclosures, goggles were not supplied for those operating grinding wheels, and such seemingly trivial injuries as splinters and cuts from broken windows often had grave consequences because of infection.

The Lyman Mills casualties from 1895 to 1916 included 1 known fatality, amputations of 5 hands, 36 fingers, and 6 toes. Injuries described in the reports as "flesh wounds" could have meant anything from the permanent incapacity of a hand to some trivial abrasion.

The Lyman Mills injury rates can be compared with those of

other cotton mills with respect to the premiums charged by the liability insurer. The American Mutual Liability Insurance Company charged a premium of forty cents per hundred dollars in wages during the last half year under the Employers' Liability law and eighty-five cents per hundred dollars during the first six months under the new Workmen's Compensation law. The fact that the premiums were the same for various mills implies that the risk was comparable and that the experience of the Lyman Mills workers can be taken as representative of the industry.[5] Other published accident analyses support the representativeness of the Lyman Mills casualty rates. Among these is a study of one thousand accidents that occurred at the Pacific Mills in Lawrence, Massachusetts from 1900 to 1905,[6] with similar rates of attribution of contributory negligence. Another compilation, though less detailed, of 3,140 textile mill injuries in New York State from 1901 to 1905 was published by Frederick L. Hoffman, along with a comparison of textile and other industries in the United Kingdom from 1900 to 1903.[7]

At Lyman Mills the distribution of injuries among workers in various mill areas shows that some departments were more hazardous than others. For the male labor force, the carding rooms, shop and yard jobs, and the cloth room were the sites of a disproportionate number of casualties, while for women the carding rooms were the most hazardous. There were no women in the shop and yard force, and only one injury to a woman was recorded in the cloth room from 1895 to 1912. Thus some of the most dangerous spots were reserved for male employees.

In the carding rooms, picker hands, strippers, card grinders, and speeder tenders appeared frequently in the injury reports. In the cloth room the job classifications of winder, folder, and shear tender accounted for numerous casualties, and in the maintenance shop carpenters led the list of injured workers.

Table 8 indicates that this pattern of injuries was clear-cut. The differences in occurrence of injuries were statistically significant at the .001 level (that is, the odds are more than a thousand to one against such a pattern being found as a random occurrence).

In each department where both men and women were employed, men were overrepresented among the casualties, or in other words, the proportion of men among the casualties exceeded the proportion of men in the departmental work force to the extent that the probability of this happening as a random occurrence was very small. This pattern is apparent in Table 9.

Though it may be argued that women are more careful than men and that an evolutionary advantage accrues to societies that are more protective of females than of males, the most

TABLE 8. *Lyman Mills Injuries By Department, 1895–1912*

	Males				
Department	Injuries Observed	Percentage	Injuries Expected[*]	Percentage	Percentage Over- or Underrepresented[†]
Carding	114	27.8	69	16.8	+65.2
Spinning	94	22.9	112	27.4	−16.1
Dressing	13	3.2	25	6.1	−48.0
Weaving	53	12.9	136	33.2	−61.0
Cloth Room	46	11.2	13	3.1	+253.8
Shop & Yard	90	22.0	55	13.4	+63.6
	410	100.0	410	100.0	
$X^2 = 194.7$ df = 5 p<.001					

	Females				
Carding	107	55.2	35	18.0	+205.7
Spinning	12	6.2	30	15.5	−60.0
Dressing	3	1.5	24	12.6	−87.5
Weaving	71	36.6	101	51.9	−29.7
Cloth Room	1	0.5	4	2.0	−75.0
	194	100.0	194	100.0	
$X^2 = 188.4$ df = 4 p<.001					

SOURCE: Lyman Mills Papers, Vols. LAC2–LAC10. Manuscript Collection, Baker Library, Harvard University, Cambridge, Mass.
  [*] The expected frequency is that number of accidents in each department proportional to the percent of the total work force found in each department.
  [†] Percentage by which observed accident frequency differs from the expected frequency.

TABLE 9. *Lyman Mills Injuries by Department and Sex Differences, 1895–1912*

Department	Injuries Observed		Injuries Expected [*]		Percentage Male Over-representation[†]	X²	p
	Male	Female	Male	Female			
Carding	114	107	91 (41.2%)	130 (58.8%)	25.3	9.8	<.01
Spinning	94	12	61 (57.2%)	45 (42.8%)	54.1	42.4	<.001
Dressing	13	3	4 (26.9%)	12 (73.1%)	200.0	24.0	<.001
Weaving	53	71	40 (32.4%)	84 (67.6%)	110.0	6.1	<.02
Cloth Room	46	1	26 (54.5%)	21 (45.5%)	76.9	35.7	<.001
Shop & Yard	90	—	90 (100.0%)	—	—	—	—
Entire Mill	410	194	312 (51.6%)	292 (48.4%)	31.4	64.1	<.001

SOURCE: Lyman Mills Papers, vols. LAC2–LAC10, Manuscript Collection, Baker Library, Harvard University, Cambridge, Mass.
[*] Cases that would have occurred if male and female injuries were sustained in the same proportion as the sex ratio of the work force.
[†] Percentage by which the observed male injury frequency exceeds the expected male injury frequency.

plausible explanation of these data is simply that it was standard personnel practice to assign the most dangerous jobs to men and boys.

In addition to the declining trend in imputation of negligence, the documents examined make it possible to discern social patterns in the distribution of negligence charges among the Lyman Mills labor force. These accusations were not randomly made against injured workers irrespective of their job classification, demographic characteristics, or cause of injury. It will be demonstrated that differentials did indeed exist in the proportion of injuries involving negligence charges, and these differentials were associated with demographic, organizational, and technological factors.

A pattern seems to emerge from Lyman Mills records that shows adolescent workers incurred significantly more charges of carelessness than adult workers. However, upon closer examination the relationship between age and cause of accident appears to be spurious. When production department data are separated from those of the shop and yard, the difference in injury rate between adolescent and adult workers, though still in the predicted direction, becomes so small as to be dismissed as a random variation (see Table 10).

TABLE 10. *Lyman Mills Injuries, 1895–1912: Age and Contributory Negligence*

Contributory Negligence Charged	Incidence of Employee Injury by Age				X^2	p
	14–17 Number	Percentage	18 & over Number	Percentage		
All Workers						
Yes	86	(69.4%)	266	(55.2%)	8.16	<.01
No	38	(30.6%)	216	(44.8%)		
	124	(100.0%)	482	(100.0%)		
Production Workers						
Yes	85	(70.2%)	258	(65.0%)	.87	NS
No	36	(29.8%)	139	(35.0%)		
	121	(100.0%)	397	(100.0%)		
Shop and Yard Force						
Yes	1	(33.3%)	8	(9.4%)	Fisher's Exact p = .262	
No	2	(66.7%)	77	(90.6%)		
	3	(100.0%)	85	(100.0%)		

SOURCE: Lyman Mills Papers, vols. LAC2–LAC10, Manuscript Collection, Baker Library, Harvard University, Cambridge, Mass.

The problem with age is further confounded when statistics of the three largest production departments are each examined independently. In the carding rooms, the proportion of injuries in which carelessness was charged is *significantly greater* among adult workers than in cases involving adolescent workers. (In the 14 to 17 age bracket, negligence was charged in 15 of 26 cases or 57.7 percent; for those aged 18 and older, negligence was charged in 160 of 210 cases or 76.2 percent; X^2 = 4.18, p < .05.) In the spinning rooms, the pattern occurs in the opposite direction with the proportion of adult workers accused of carelessness *significantly smaller* than injured adolescents. (In the 14 to 17 age bracket, 66 of 77 injury cases were accused of carelessness or 88.0 percent; for those aged 18 and older, 23 of 33 cases or 69.7 percent; X^2 = 5.29, p < .05.) In the weaving rooms, there was no significant difference in this respect, but only 4.3 percent of 117 injuries to weaving personnel involved workers under the age of eighteen.

As shown in Table 9, women suffered proportionately fewer injuries than men in all Lyman Mills departments that employed both women and men. Any inference that women were subjected proportionately to fewer charges of contributory negligence, however, is not borne out by examination of the data. On the face of it, the opposite appears to have been the case, because 65.5 percent of injured women were charged with carelessness as compared with only 53.6 percent of injured men and boys. This seemingly paradoxical pattern is, in fact, spurious, because when the all-male shop and yard force is excluded, the proportion for males is 65.3 percent, virtually the same as for women.

A departmental breakdown showed one exception to the pattern in the spinning rooms, where a significantly higher proportion of injuries to males than to females was followed by imputation of carelessness. The spinning work force included, however, a large proportion of young boys who not only had the most dangerous jobs but were taxed almost invariably for contributory negligence.

The shop and yard force, though overrepresented among the male casualties, was significantly underrepresented in the proportion of cases involving charges of carelessness. From 1895 to 1912, 335 of 528 injuries in the production departments (63.8 percent) were so labeled, while only 10 of 87 injuries in the shop and yard force (11.5 percent) involved such accusations ($X^2 = 82.82$, $p < .001$). A plausible explanation of this discrepancy is that the shop and yard force, particularly the carpenters, millwrights, and machinists, had the most skilled jobs in the mill which were also some of the most hazardous given the prevailing state of the industrial arts. These circumstances led to a high incidence of wounds and a reluctance to level accusations of carelessness in these cases because of the seeming contradiction in accusing the most highly skilled workers of being careless and irresponsible.

During the period of this study, massive immigration occurred, and many recruits to the industrial labor force at that time were unable to speak English.[8] The heavy toll of industrial casualties was often attributed to the language problems of the "greenhorns." At the Lyman Mills from 1895 to 1912, 47.7 percent of all injuries were incurred by workers unable to speak English. Excluding the shop and yard force, among whom only 4.5 percent of the casualties were non-English speakers, in the remaining production departments the proportion of injured workers unable to speak English was 55.0 percent.

One of the presuppositions of this study was that employees unable to understand work instructions given in English would be overrepresented among those accused of contributory negligence. Though 47.7 percent of all casualties were non-English speakers, among the 352 cases in which contributory negligence was imputed, 61.1 percent were unable to communicate in the dominant tongue. Table 11 develops this analysis and shows that this relationship between language and accusations of carelessness holds true for production as well as shop and yard workers.

The only exception to this pattern was in the adolescent work force, among whom 31.5 percent of the casualties were non-English speaking. While three-fourths of the non-English speakers in the 14 to 17 age bracket injured, as compared with two-thirds of the·English speakers in the same age bracket, were charged with contributory negligence, this difference, though in the expected direction, was not statistically significant. Only among the youngest workers, then, was language not significantly related to the imputation of contributory negligence.

Thus, ability or inability to communicate in English was an important factor in the unequal contest over injury costs. Recent immigrants from non-English speaking countries were less likely to recover damages under the liability law than Americans or English-speaking immigrants. It is not possible to determine whether inability to understand supervisory in-

TABLE 11. *Lyman Mills Injuries, 1895–1912: Language and Contributory Negligence*

	Contributory Negligence Charged	English-speaking Workers				X^2	p
		Yes		No			
		Number	Percentage	Number	Percentage		
All Workers	Yes	137	(43.2%)	215	(74.4%)	60.01	<.001
	No	180	(56.8%)	74	(25.6%)		
		317	(100.0%)	289	(100.0%)		
Production	Yes	131	(56.2%)	212	(74.4%)	19.45	<.001
Departments	No	102	(43.8%)	73	(25.6%)		
		233	(100.0%)	285	(100.0%)		
Shop and	Yes	6	(7.1%)	3	(75.0%)	[Fisher's	
Yard Force	No	78	(92.9%)	1	(25.0%)	Exact	
		84	(100.0%)	4	(100.0%)	p = .003]	
Age 18 &	Yes	79	(34.3%)	185	(74.3%)	77.22	< .001
over	No	151	(65.7%)	64	(25.7%)		
		230	(100.0%)	249	(100.0%)		
Age 14–17	Yes	58	(66.7%)	30	(75.0%)	.91	NS
	No	29	(33.3%)	10	(25.0%)		
		87	(100.0%)	40	(100.0%)		

SOURCE: Lyman Mills Papers, Vols. LAC2–LAC10. Manuscript Collection, Baker Library, Harvard University, Cambridge, Mass.

structions and attendant failure to work safely accounted for greater likelihood of non-English speakers being accused of carelessness, or whether the seemingly endless stream of immigrants encouraged employers to treat foreigners as expendables to be assigned to the most dangerous jobs and to be written off as cheaply as possible when injured. Nevertheless, it is very probable that both of these factors were interwoven in creating this disadvantage for the foreign language speakers. In addition, newcomers who had only the most tenuous roots in a community and with a narrower range of alternative opportunities than those available to native-born people would be reluctant to "make trouble" in the face of unfair treatment.

Length of service in the mill is another variable that one would expect to be related to the injury patterns. In the absence of seniority data on the mill population as a whole, it is possible only to compare the length of service of injured workers charged with contributory negligence and those who were not charged. Though the differences are not statistically significant, they occur in the expected direction, that is, workers charged with carelessness tend to have shorter periods of employment than those not charged. This expectation rests on the supposition that those who are least able to adapt to the constraints of the mill will be selected out and that a learning process takes place over time in which those who endure come to know at least in part how to avoid situations in which they may be taxed for carelessness.

Of course, length of service is not independent of age; one cannot accumulate experience without getting older. Despite the seemingly spurious relationship between age and contributory negligence, there seems to be a patterned relationship between length of service and imputation of contributory negligence. Of injuries to production workers in which allegations of contributory negligence appear in the record, 49.2 percent occurred during the first ninety days of service in the mill. In cases in which negligence was not charged, only 42.6 percent occurred during the first ninety days (83/321 of the former and 39/176 of the latter, $X^2 = 1.98$, $.20 > p > .10$). Estimated median length of service was 91 days in cases where carelessness was charged and 140 days in cases where it was not. Furthermore, for all production workers' injuries between 1895 and 1912, 10.9 percent occurred within the first seven days of employment and 22.4 percent before the end of the first month. Clearly, being new on the job compounded the danger to the employee, in part because of inexperience and in part from a personnel practice of placing new people on the worst jobs. The latter practice can be attributed to a certain extent to the probability that the worst jobs had the greatest turnover.

It is also of interest to determine whether any patterned differences in imputation of contributory negligence were associated with different causes of injury. This analysis is based on

532 injury cases in Lyman Mills production departments from 1895 to 1912, using those injuries recorded by causes. Table 12 indicates that 75.7 percent of injuries brought about by involvement with moving machinery and elevators were attributed to carelessness, while only 25.8 percent of the casualties resulting from flying shuttles and falling objects were so charged. Falls and the remaining category of "miscellaneous" injuries both were marked by contributory negligence charges in just under one half of the cases.

The standard accusation of carelessness in cases where workers' hands were caught while trying to remove waste from moving machinery "contrary to instructions" fails to take into account the inevitable pressures to maximize production and the toll taken by fatigue on the workers' alertness.

The much lower proportion of contributory negligence charges in accidents involving falling objects and loose shuttles compared to accidents from other causes can be explained. When workers were injured by shuttles flying out of a loom because the yarn broke it would have strained the credulity of the most hard-hearted juror to claim that these victims were somehow the authors of their own misfortune.

In the case of injuries from falls, the assessment of circumstances varied. A worker who fell into a trap door left unguarded by maintenance personnel could hardly be blamed for

TABLE 12. *Injury Sources and Contributory Negligence, Production Departments. 1895–1912*

Injury Source	Total Injuries	Charged with Contributory Negligence	
		Number	Percentage
Machinery and Elevators	362	274	(75.7%)
Shuttles and Falling Objects	62	16	(25.8%)
Falls	32	15	(46.9%)
Miscellaneous	76	37	(48.7%)
TOTAL	532	342	(64.3%)

SOURCE: Lyman Mills Papers, Vols. LAC2–LAC10. Manuscript Collection, Baker Library, Harvard University, Cambridge, Mass.

his injury. In such a case the fellow servant rule could be invoked. In a case where a woman broke her leg when she slipped and fell in the mill yard the insurer stated that "she knew or should have known" that the walkway would be icy in February, and she was blamed for her injury. In the remaining miscellaneous category, which included cuts or abrasions from metal objects, broken glass, or emery dust; and burns, wood splinters, and others, no discernible pattern was found comparable to that found among the injuries involving machinery and elevators or shuttles and falling objects.

When the 1887 Massachusetts Employers' Liability Law[9] was replaced by "no-fault" compensation, which took effect in July 1912,[10] accusations of negligence no longer saved money for the employer. Examination of injury reports reveals that, as a result of the legislation, the proportion of contributory negligence cases to total cases differs dramatically, before and after the July 1912 inauguration of Workmen's Compensation.

The Lyman Mills did not immediately become a safer place to work following the enactment of the no-fault work injury law. The 1908–11 average of 35.5 injury reports per year is comparable with the 1913–16 average of 39.2 per year. In contrast, there was a statistically significant reduction in the proportion of cases in which injury was attributed to the victim's carelessness. For the period from January 1895 to July 1912, of 611 recorded injuries, 345 were connected with accusations of carelessness (56.5 percent). Beginning with the first case under the Workmen's Compensation law in July 1912 through the end of 1916, 40 of 176 cases (22.7 percent) were taxed with contributory negligence ($X^2 = 61.97$, p<.001). In 1911, 52.8 percent of the Lyman injury reports includes an accusation of carelessness, as opposed to 17.6 percent in 1912.

For comparison we may look to the injury reports of the Lawrence Manufacturing Company, a large cotton mill in Lowell, Massachusetts. Here during the first six months of 1912, 84.5 percent of injuries were attributed to carelessness, while during the last six months of 1912—after the new law went into effect—only 12.2 percent of the case records include accusations of carelessness or violation of instructions. It can be seen from these documents that beginning in July 1912, there was a remarkable reduction in imputation of contributory negligence.

The injury records of the Lyman Mills reveal the nature and distribution of injuries in this factory during the period in our industrial development when work-related casualties reached their peak. The data also show patterns in the imputation of contributory negligence, an employer defense against liability claims under the law that preceded Workmen's Compensation. These patterns were associated with demographic factors such as age, sex, English-speaking ability, and skill, as well as with differences among mill departments.

After the no-fault Workmen's Compensation law went into effect, the number of injuries remained at the same level as before, but there was a significantly lower proportion of cases in which the injury was blamed on victim carelessness. There is no reason to suppose that in 1912 mill employees suddenly became more careful. It seems more likely that charges of contributory negligence had often reflected nothing more than an expedient manner for employers to avoid liability for work injuries, and under the new law there was no advantage to be derived from such allegations.

In the relationships of the workplace there are obvious disparities in power. These disparities were reflected in the Lyman Mills accident record. By state intervention, changes in the laws governing the treatment of work casualties affected the disparities in the power relations in the factory. The new Workmen's Compensation legislation eliminated the scandalous practice of sending the great majority of work casualties away empty-handed. In substituting no-fault insurance for the draconian liability statutes that preceded it, the state injected a measure of rationality into industrial relations and made the conflict over work hazards less one-sided.

CHAPTER 4

Adversaries, Third Parties, and Work Injuries

IN 1902 the resident agent in charge of a cotton mill in Chicopee, Massachusetts informed the company's liability insurer of his progress in dealing with two injury cases resulting from the malfunctioning of an elevator. "I am trying the Chicopee method of settlement, i.e., waiting till they get hungry for money before going to see them."[1] There is, of course, no need to suppose that the Chicopee method was peculiar to this locality in anything but name. To pay as little as possible to victims of work injuries was, then as now, a perfectly rational strategy for managers constrained by the imperative of minimizing costs. The priority of putting cost control over injury compensation does not enhance the public image of industry, and it should come as no surprise that the relevant records in operating enterprises are inaccessible. Thus historical data on factory injuries are doubly valuable because they shed light on past practice and provide a basis for inference about present conditions.

Correspondence between the resident agent of the Dwight Manufacturing Company and the liability insurer reveals the complex network of adversary relations and third-party influence in the process of apportioning the costs of mill injuries. Letters dating from 1897 to 1912 are the data source for this chapter.

Since more for one party necessarily means less for the other, settlement of injury cases was approached by the management with the intention of minimizing payments and dissuading workers who might resort to litigation. The correspondence with the insurer concerning these settlements displayed an epistolary style punctuated by gratuitous expressions of contempt. This antagonistic relationship is demonstrated by an exchange between Annie Cronin and the mill agent. When she called to inquire about insurance payments, the manager responded: "I asked her how she injured her hand and she said she 'didn't know, but thought she must have slipped and, trying to save herself, threw her hand against the belt.' Told her that I could do nothing for her, as the company was not in any way responsible. . . . The people about here seem to think that the Dwight Company is a charitable institution. Think this will be a good chance to undeceive them" (HL1, 3/14/98).

The adversary nature of the bargaining that took place with injury victims was expressed in another case by the insurer: "If he likes to take $10 and give you a release, we will allow that; if not, let him try what he can make at law and we will defend you" (ML3, 3/4/10). In another instance, the mill agent (plant manager) reported that the company had offered to pay a worker's hospital bill and added that the worker was given the impression that "we were very generous" (HL1, 3/21/98). The tone of the letter provides the inescapable conclusion that the pretense of generosity was deliberately deceptive.

When an injured worker signed a release and left town, the management's relief epitomizes the dehumanization of working people, as if it were a matter of discarding a damaged factor of production. The attitude was that it was better if the disabled worker went far away rather than stay to demand work suitable to his condition or to become a burden on the taxpayers. "Inclosed find report of accident to Wm. Knapp, [who had fallen into an elevator shaft] also release signed from same party. Got clear of this case very nicely as he has already taken train for his native town in New York state. . . . Wm. Szetela . . . was in today, and I finally made settlement with him for

$45. His hand will always be rigid, so that he cannot obtain employment readily, therefore intends to go back to Poland." (HL1, 11/6/99; 7/10/01).

The employer's desire to avoid litigation was a common theme. The certainty of a signed release—if the worker was a legal adult—was preferable to the uncertain outcome of a trial under the Employers' Liability Law, especially in the face of rising juror sympathy for plaintiffs injured in the mills. Intervention of skilled advocates on the workers' side was a contingency to be avoided.

> Succeeded in getting Mr. Robinson and effected a settlement with him for $60. As you surmised he was approached by a lawyer of this place, who advised him to attach the Company for $7500. After talking the matter over with him a little while, succeeded in making settlement. . . . offered Glasky's wife $25.00 in settlement of the case, but she refused, so that probably the next thing will be a notice from the "German lawyer" in Holyoke. [HL 2, 10/22/04; 4/28/06]

The insurer's letters also attest to the conflict of adversaries. One worker's hospital bill was large, and the opinion of the insurer was that "we think it ought not to be paid in full, unless there is some reason to apprehend that he could recover damages of you at law" (ML32, 2/9/98). When the outcome of litigation seemed predictably to be in favor of the plaintiff, the insurer advised that "we do not want a suit . . . if we can avoid it at a reasonable price" (ML30, 9/13/97).

The process was sometimes affected by a threat of court action. A worker who demanded $200 for a permanently incapacitated hand rejected the employer's offer of $50 and proposed to sue. His interpreter told the company: "Well, we will have to do something else, as we could not consider such a small sum" (HL2, 1/8/07). This threat of doing "something else," that is, litigation, raised the company's offer to $100, which was accepted. Some workers rejected such compromise offers, and in view of their weak bargaining position their courage seems admirable. In the case of Bridget Linehan, the agent wrote to the insurer: "I can settle with her . . . by paying her time and Drs. bill. . . . Tried to beat her down, but she said she would not take a cent less" (HL3, 3/31/08). She was twenty-four years old, had been employed in the mill for eight years, and was injured by a lever of the machine she operated when a loose nut caused the lever to slip. She went to her family doctor rather than the company doctor. Several weeks before the candid, though injudicious, admission that he had tried to beat her down, the agent reported to the insurer Bridget Linehan's claim that "since she was injured through no carelessness of her own . . . 'she thinks it the duty of the company to pay her wages and expenses.' What shall I tell her?" (HL3, 3/10/08). Linehan seemed well versed in the law and unwilling to be beaten down. More often than not, however, the resistance of the casualties could be worn down by the "Chicopee method."

On occasion the insurer praised management for finesse in applying this method: "You have at last succeeded in making a settlement with Mike George. . . . This is very satisfactory, as we did not expect to get rid of him without a suit" (ML39, 9/11/06). George had refused a payment of $15, after which the insurer raised the allowable sum to $50. Instead, the agent obtained a settlement for $40. This was standard procedure. Concerning a take-it-or-leave-it offer to Annie Kelly, the insurer wrote to the mill agent: "We give you limit of $50 to settle the case. . . . You will of course get off for as much less as you can. Do not pay anything without a release. . . . [If she rejects it we shall] make a fight; and she cannot . . . expect you to employ her and thus supply her with funds for suing you" (ML36, 4/20/05; ML37, 8/22/05).

There is also evidence that efforts were made to deny the injured workers and their representatives, if any, access to evidence that might support their claim for damages. The Dwight agent was cautioned by the insurer: "Do not allow [the attorney] or anyone else representing the boy to enter your works for the purpose of examining the machine where the boy was injured" (ML36, 3/15/04). After an accident caused by a defective chain hoist the same insurer instructed the management of another mill to let nobody examine the broken chain links. Thus concealment of evidence was a part of the adversary struggle over apportionment of injury costs.

When the employer became aware of the probability of future medical complications, he was not averse to getting a quick release signed by the victim, who presumably was not privy to the prognosis made by the company doctor. Thus the Dwight agent wrote to the insurer that, "we made settlement with Powall Sheizer for $60 and we enclose release signed by him. . . . It developed that one of the metacarpal bones was broken and some of it came out. It is possible that more of it may come out later. . . . If it does, it may cause him more trouble, but we thought it best to settle with him" (HL4, 7/10/11).

A physician faithful to the Hippocratic oath or a good shop steward would have cautioned Sheizer against signing the release. Management tactics in the adversary process clearly did not preclude deception, if deception was expedient for minimizing costs.

The company doctor and the worker's family doctor, then as now, entered the arena of industrial conflict as third parties on the side of one or the other adversary. The injured worker was at a disadvantage because he often lacked the means and the opportunity to take issue with the medical decisions bought and paid for by the company.

In this sense, Parsons's description of the medical therapist as "a prototype of the mechanism of social control"[2] seems appropriate. The physician who is employed to patch up the casualties and get them back to work at minimum cost provides a service to the employer in which any benefit to the patient is incidental.

Availability of medical care provided by an agent of the patient or a neutral source may redress the balance somewhat, a prospect often displeasing to the employer. Modern-day managers also complain that the convalescence of workers left to the ministrations of their family physicians tends to be longer than when decisions are made by the company doctor. Even now, many industrial workers perceive the company doctor as an adversary.

In the Dwight mills the case of Mary Dunn is particularly instructive. She went to a doctor not beholden to the company, and his professional judgment was maligned by the mill agent (a layman).

This girl went to a young Doctor of this place (Dr. Gates) to be treated. . . . He reported that . . . he thought she had received a slight concussion of the brain. . . . The report also states that there was no mark discernible, so that everything indicates "fake," even to the physicians' report; the latter grew indignant when writer suggested that his examination found more than actually existed. [HL2, 10/14/04]

The company doctor said that Mary Dunn's health was as good as his own and expressed willingness to testify under oath that there was no indication of a concussion. "He calls it a 'fake,' pure and simple" (HL2, 10/18/04).

Often another kind of professional judgment was rendered when injured mill workers were left to the tender mercies of the company doctors. The Dwight Papers relate the case of an employee whose hand was mangled in the machinery. "We sent him to *our* surgeon, who now reports that the hand is an excellent job from a surgical stand-point, but that he does not think Michael will have the use of any of the fingers" (HL2, 1/3/07; emphasis supplied).

There were numerous instances when the insurer refused to pay the doctor's bill unless the injured employee was treated by the company doctor. In one case, the insurer suspected that the employee would "probably be instigated by her doctor to make trouble. . . . We . . . recommend you to employ at once a doctor of good standing in Chicopee to make an examination. . . . Although the claim is probably a fraud we fear that a Jury may give her something. Therefore if you see an opportunity to settle . . . for a small amount notify us promptly" (ML39,

10/15/06; 10/26/06). Physicians participated on both sides in the encounter of adversaries, but the preponderance of medical resources was on the employer's side.

The interpreter was an important third-party figure in the struggle over work injuries in the Dwight mills in the decades that bracketed the turn of the century. The question of translation is not a simple one of rendering a statement from one language to another. Disparities in social rank enter the situation, and it can be seen quite clearly from the Dwight mills documents that a great deal depended upon *whose agent* the interpreter happened to be in any given case. The outcome varied, depending on whether the injured worker had the services of an interpreter who sided with him or whether the linguistic mediation was controlled by management.

The effectiveness of the worker's "own" interpreter was noted, as on one occasion when the agent wrote to the insurer about an injured employee who "had a different interpreter this time—one who appeared much sharper and brighter than the ordinary Polish interpreter" (HL1, 3/21/98). Clearly, when the linguistic intermediary was not an agent of the company, it benefitted management if he was not too "bright."

On another occasion the management wrote about the services of interpreters who were on the company's side and yet collected a fee from workers in whose cases they appeared:

We consider that we were fortunate in getting these terms with them, as they were both beset with "shyster lawyers" who were anxious to take the case, and sue for large amounts as they thought they had a clear case against the Company, but with the aid of the interpreters who were friendly to us (one of them was paid by Sliva himself out of the $200) we succeeded in persuading them to accept the amounts offered. [HL2, 3/21/02]

Some of the letters refer to one particular interpreter who was active from 1909 to 1912. They shed some light on what was essentially a staff service in personnel management rendered by an outside contractor on a fee-for-service basis. It may be supposed that there was a double benefit for the employer in this arrangement. First, there was no need to pay a regular salary but only an interpreter's fee when the need arose, which could be passed on to the liability insurer as part of the cost of settling an injury case. Secondly, the interpreter, in an ostensibly independent position, could more readily win the confidence of (and thus deceive) the worker, than if he were a member of the mill management. "Paul Starzyk, who acted as interpreter in the above case, called us up . . . and inquired if he was to get something out of it. . . . In making the settlement, the woman evidently thought the amount was small, but after talking the matter over . . . with Mr. Starzyk, she finally said she would not bother with it any more, and would settle for that amount" (HL3, 2/17/10).

It was also apparent that bargaining over the interpreter's fee was part of the allocation of accident costs. Whenever a worker who was unable to speak English was dissuaded from litigation or persuaded to accept a low settlement, the interpreter earned his keep.

Paul Starzyk, who is acting as interpreter for Swavick, telephoned us . . . that the latter would not accept $10.00 in settlement, but thinks if your man should be here . . . he could arrange a settlement at a low figure, although parties have been trying to get this man to give his case to a Springfield lawyer, who is said to *buy* them at a good figure. We settled this morning with Apolina Dejato . . . for $20 and enclose release signed by her. Mr. Starzyk thinks he ought to have a little remuneration for persuading her to settle at this figure and her hand is still in pretty bad condition. [HL3, 8/8/10; 2/12/11]

The potential for gain by threatening to change sides in the adversary relationship did not escape Starzyk's notice. In one case a representative of the insurance company offended him, and he threatened thereafter to fan the flames of litigiousness instead of quenching them.

Regarding Mr. Starzyk, your Mr. Kinney stirred him a good deal . . . and he feels pretty sore and undoubtedly will take sides against the Company and advise people who come to him to see a lawyer instead of, as he has been doing, advising them to settle. . . . He says he will get more money out of it in such cases. In this present case, he came here at least four times . . . and think [*sic*] that he should have some consideration for advising them to settle even for this amount ($150), as their first amount was $700 and he is sure they would get much more than $150 if lawyers pressed the matter for them. [HL4, 7/11/11]

Only four days later it was made apparent that he found it prudent to stay on management's side and continue to bargain for his fees. "We succeeded in getting Mr. Starzyk to influence Andrew Mikus to sign a release for $140 which we enclose to you. We thought this would furnish $10 for Mr. Starzyk but he thinks he ought to get $15" (HL4, 7/15/11). The insurer considered the interpreter's demand to be extravagant, but authorized payment "for the sake of peace" (ML44, 7/18/11). The versatility of this particular interpreter was evidenced a year later when, after one of the fatal accidents in the Dwight mill, it was he who submitted a bill for $14.85 to defray the cost of a burial suit for the victim.

Like the employer, the insurer sought to minimize costs and the fee-for-service interpreter posed something of a dilemma. "We authorize you to make an allowance not exceeding $5 to the interpreter Starzyk. You will please consider carefully . . . whether this is prudent. If the interpreter gets an allowance in this way it may encourage him to take up claims; on the other hand the effect may be that he will be more ready to settle cases reasonably when they come into his hands" (ML44, 12/4/11). Interpreters were needed so long as newly-arrived immigrants comprised a large part of the work force, and men like Starzyk, in furnishing a necessary service, obviously had to be paid.

After enactment of Workmen's Compensation, the Massachusetts Industrial Accident Board hired its own interpreters because "certain interpreters were exploiting for their own benefit injured employees and their dependents" and because "frequently one side or the other objected to the interpreting of evidence by an interpreter engaged and paid for by the opposing party."[3]

The preference of the management for doctors, interpreters, lawyers, and public officials friendly to the employer's interests seems reasonable enough when friendship is seen as a resource and a basis of power advantage. Conversely, there was an unconcealed eagerness to isolate the victims from such friends as might instigate litigation. For example, the mill agent reported to the insurer after one settlement: "This is the best we could do with him. But considered it for the benefit of all concerned, to get his release for this amount, rather than let him fall into the hands of his friends" (HL1, 10/10/98).

While one may think of a bona fide labor union as a valued "friend" of the worker—and there was some union activity in Chicopee during the period under study—there appears to be no evidence of any kind of shop floor organization to deal with safety matters. Nevertheless, in a few instances, there is reference to the existence of an organization: "She complains of severe headaches etc., and has some first class advice from some of her 'Union' friends, whose secretary was in to speak for her" (HL2, 4/19/02).

In the main, however, the preponderance of "friendly" third-party support in the conflict over allocation of injury costs was on the side of the employer. Management had such friends as the coroner who neglected to order an inquest into a fatal accident, the overseer of the poor who urged acceptance of a settlement offer, and the state inspector who failed to order erection of a gate in front of an elevator shaft. These were helpful to one party and detrimental to the other. Friendly doctors, lawyers, and interpreters were drawn in large measure to the privileged rather than to the deprived. Thus the Chicopee method and the whole complex of cost-cutting at the expense of injured workers rested on inequalities in the social structure.

Part of the leverage in the Chicopee method was to deny employment to injured workers who sued for damages. The insurer's letters to the company reiterate the advice: "If he persists in his claim you will have no further use of his services" (ML32, 3/17/99). "We suppose you will hardly employ her again if she makes trouble" (ML37, 5/2/05). The company readily concurred in this advice, and in one case the agent wrote about a litigious worker that Dwight Manufacturing "certainly will not give her employment while she is against us" (HL2, 3/21/02).

Another worker's statement concerning her injury, the insurer suggested, "is very cautious, probably made under legal advice; we do not believe she is telling all she knows. . . . It is most likely a scheme by the doctor to get his pay. We advise you to tell her that you recognize no legal liability and can make her no allowance. If she sues you, we will give her a good long fight, and we presume in that case you will have no further need for her in your service" (ML32, 3/18/98).

The impact of the club of unemployment over the workers' heads was far more serious than simply losing a job at the Dwight mill. Operation of a blacklist meant that workers labeled as troublemakers in one mill would be denied employment in a network of other mills whose managers kept one another informed about such matters.

The correspondence about injuries is marked by frequent mention of managerial characterization of injured workers as compliant or recalcitrant. The troublemakers were of course prime prospects for the Chicopee method. Yet one should not suppose that the men who occupied authority positions in the mill were ogres devoid of any feelings of sympathy or impulses of kindness toward some of the casualties among their subordinates.

There is much in these letters that bespeaks a cynical disregard for workers as an expendable factor of production, but the record is not unrelieved by occasional expressions of noblesse oblige toward the *deserving* poor, particularly those who had long records of faithful service and unusual hardship. From the management side, these expressions usually took the form of an appeal to the insurer. One injured weaver with many years of service "would not ask for help, had she not recently been to considerable expense owing to the death of her brother. Anything you can do for her would be appreciated" (HL2, 3/14/02). In another case, the insurer was asked to give an old "standby" some of the money that had been held back from other cases by the expedient of getting them to sign releases for less than the amount authorized by the insurer. Deserving casualties included a worker who had been in the country only seven weeks, and another who supported a wife and eight children in the "old country."

Michael Dooley, after thirty years' service, was described as "perhaps more worthy of notice than some others," but the insurer authorized a settlement for only $10. In response to company pleading on behalf of the injured employee the insurer usually commented that charity and compassion were worthy sentiments, but their cost should be defrayed by the mill owners. In the absence of legal liability, the insurers declined to make contributions to the injured, except in token amounts to secure a signed release and avert litigation. This was a kind of insurance for the insurer, since juries were unpredictable and even a successful legal defense would cost more than the $10 it cost to get an injured empoyee to sign a release. Compassion was served only so long as it was compatible with cost cutting. In one instance the insurer observed that the case could have cost more if the worker had been "properly coached by a lawyer" (ML44, 9/9/11), a statement that has less to do with generosity than with minimizing costs.

Kindness and compassion were not totally absent in the mill. The liability insurer simply rejected the cost of these noble sentiments. "Yours of July 8th is at hand respecting the case of Bridget O'Rourke. This is pretty plainly not a case of liability but only of compassion which is a very proper motive for your action, but we cannot give it much weight" (ML35, 7/9/03). The insurer, equally constrained by a goal of minimizing costs, passed the expenditures based on moral obligations back to the company and limited payment to matters covered under the terms of the Employers' Liability Law.

Since the insurer's potential profit was diminished by payments of claims, potential for conflict between insurer and insured also existed. This conflict, however, was limited by the terms of the insurance policy, which in turn reflected the provisions of the Employers' Liability Law. Disputes arose over the amounts disbursed, but the insurer's contractual liability obliged that only damages arising out of actions for negligence be absorbed. Still, there was some bargaining between the manufacturing companies and their insurers, and the documents contain expressions of dissatisfaction with the insurer. In one case the mill agent bargained over a payment of $10: "If you do not care to go in to the extent of $10 . . . why we will pay half" (HL1, 9/12/99).

In another instance the insurer's refusal to pay a hospital bill evoked a strong complaint from the agent:

We have your letter of the 11th inst. regarding Springfield Hospital bill . . . and note that you do not think it worth while to pay this bill. If you do not pay it, the Dwight Co. will have to. As before written you, we employ a doctor by the year to give first aid to all accident cases, and it is only on his judgment that cases are sent to the Hospital. In the case in question, if Bickley had not been sent to the hospital, there is no question but what it would have been a decidedly more serious case, with consequent increased liability for your Company in case of suit. We cannot see wherein his "probably poor physical condition" could have been considered at the time of the accident, as prompt measures were unquestionably demanded, but would like to have some expression from you how we are to decide in the future whether cases are to be sent to the hospital or not, regardless of the physician's judgment. [HL4, 7/12/11]

During the previous year, the insurer had advised the company that if the hospital demanded assurance of payment before admitting a patient, the solution was to find another hospital.

Two cases involving hospitalization can be compared in the context of work injury to show how medical progress outstripped the organization of health care delivery. In 1901, a worker was cut when his hand slipped while he was opening a window. Nine days later the agent notified the insurer: "We regret to inform you that lock-jaw set in . . . and terminated fatally last night" (HL1, 7/13/01). The insurer's reply was more comforting to the management than to the victim's next of kin: "This is a very unfortunate accident, but you are not responsible for it. If any claim is made, or trouble threatened, please let us know, and in the meantime incur no expense on our account" (ML34, 7/16/01).

Nine years later, in a different case, even though tetanus antitoxin had become available, the insurer demurred over the bill. The mill agent summarized the hospital's report that "after the necessary surgery was performed, Tetanus set in and in order to save his life, they gave him Anti-toxin treatment. . . . They report that the treatment has been the means of saving his life, but wish to ask whether we do not feel like helping them out on the expense of the Anti-toxin, of which they claimed to have used $200 or $300 worth" (HL3, 8/31/10). About three weeks later the agent wrote to the insurer that he had informed the hospital that the insurer "did not feel like assuming the cost of the anti-toxin." The insurer then advised Dwight Company that it would be prudent to decline payment of the hospital bill pending litigation. "If a settlement is made perhaps this hospital bill can be considered in it, but if no settlement is made there is no reason why you should pay it" (ML43, 10/24/10). Presumably if the case went to trial and the plaintiff lost, the hospital would be obliged to recover from the patient. In most cases, this in effect would leave the hospital with an unpaid bill.

It may seem ironic, but not surprising, that the liability insurer sought to beat down not only injured claimants but also the insurer's own legal representatives. The cover letter accompanying a payment of $20 for services in an injury case stated: "We fully appreciate the value of your learning and experience in difficult and important cases, and are quite willing to pay accordingly, but for little things of this kind, which can be attended to by one lawyer as well as another, we cannot afford to pay so much, and it would perhaps be better for us to turn them over to some one whose time is less valuable."

The reply of the learned counselor must have been an angry one because it elicited a prompt and conciliatory rejoinder only three days later.

I am fully convinced that you are a valuable friend of the Co. and I want to make the connection mutually profitable—I don't like to question bills of any sort and least of all those of professional men who don't get what they deserve in this world as compared with all the ignorant tradesmen and stock-brokers. Only I feel called upon to save money for the Co. when I can—we are by no means a bloated corporation & have to conduct our business carefully & charge low premiums to meet a lively competition.[4]

Thus, while the Chicopee method exemplified the minimizing of payment by one class to another, the existence of intraclass conflict is demonstrated by the insurance company manager's attempt to minimize the payment to the company's attorney.

The ramifications of the Chicopee method are illustrated in the case of Victoria Guyette, a thirty-two-year old weaver. In the summer of 1901, a broken thread caused a shuttle to fly out of a loom and hit her in the sternum, "slightly fracturing the tip end of it, causing a lump to form and she afterwards vomited some blood" (HL1, 7/23/01). There could be no imputation of contributory negligence, but the conflict over payment lasted over two months, a time span of sufficient duration for the managerial stratagem of "waiting till they get hungry" to come into play.

The correspondence concerning this case and its outcome is indicative of the role of third parties in injury disputes, and it illuminates the deceptive practices commonly used against injury victims. Concerning Guyette the agent wrote:

[I] wish to say that the injury she received will confine her to bed a week or two longer, and the Doctor reports that better food and less worry on her part would improve matters. She has two small children and receives no assistance from her husband. . . . Mrs. Guyette claims that the loom was out of order, also that she had called the fixer's attention to it. . . . Think therefore that she might receive encouragement to put in a claim. [HL1, 8/6/01]

The insurer's first response was to set a limit of $25, including doctor's bills, to settle the case. The Dwight Manufacturing Company agent replied that this was insufficient: "We tried all along to have her feel that the Company would do what is right, but her ideas were far above anything we could offer her" (HL1, 8/16/01). A month after the accident she applied for public assistance and her "caseworker" entered the process as a third party on the side of the employer:

The overseer of the Poor called here before going to see her today and I suggested to him that he advise her to settle. He reported later that he thought some sort of settlement might be made with her, if gone about in a proper way. He further said that he had explained to her that she was acting foolish . . . in bringing a suit, that the lawyers would get it, and that it would be for her benefit to keep out of their clutches. [HL1, 8/23/01]

Though it is of course true that lawyers who took up liability cases for injured workers on a contingent fee basis had to charge enough in the cases they won to cover their expenses in the cases they lost, the facts seem to indicate that the caseworker was more concerned with minimizing the employer's and the taxpayer's expense than with the well-being of his client. Notwithstanding his advice, Victoria Guyette filed a law suit. Impending litigation led to increased pressure on her to come to terms. The agent sent his mill superintendent to see her:

Mr. Simpson, while strolling by her abode, *happened* to see her sitting in the doorway, and stopped to speak to her. . . . After talking and sympathizing with her awhile, he suggested that she call at his office and see what arrangements I would make with her. . . . He told her it would be much better for her to settle now and avoid paying large lawyers fees, that she would receive but a little of it, should they win the case, and that your Company would fight to the bitter

end etc. After talking with her quite a while, he thought she would
be inclined to settle for from $400 to $500. He told her that it would
be best for her to come and see me, at the same time *giving her the
impression that he was urging this without my knowledge, for her
sake*, etc. [HL1, 9/11/01; emphasis supplied]

The mill manager tried also to secure a medical opinion favorable to the company position, but the physician in the case
declined to render it, saying that "he had not made sufficient
examination to satisfy himself that Aneurism would not take
place" (HL1, 9/11/01). On the following day, the insurer raised
the settlement allowance to $50. Toward the end of the month,
the caseworker suggested "that $100 about might effect a set-
tlement. Her friends, however, advise her to fight, still I am of
the opinion that if she could be approached by someone who
had authority to 'increase the limit a little,' a satisfactory settlement might be made. Understand she is again sick in bed"
(HL1, 9/28/01). The insurance company then raised the limit
to $125 and the Dwight agent reported back that he had "fi-
nally succeeded in making a settlement" for that amount, "although at one time it looked as if a larger amount would have
to be offered her" (HL1, 10/2/01).

The adversary relationship between employer and injured
worker, bargaining between insurer and insured, the subser-
vience of town government to the mill interests, and the use of
deception to minimize the company's cost are documented in
this case. The communications between the mill management
and the liability insurer support the conclusion that the men
adept in the Chicopee method enjoyed remarkable success.

The goal of the employer and insurer alike was to secure a
signed release from the injured employee in order to close the
case. When the casualties were unable to speak English, care
was taken to have the signing witnessed by an interpreter
friendly to management, who could be relied upon to testify
that the terms of the settlement were fully explained in the na-

tive language of the injured worker. This was necessary to avoid subsequent charges of fraud.

In the case of minors, a release could be repudiated when the signer came of age. Parental signatures were binding against suit by the injured minor's parent and constrained the child from court action only if the parent was a court-appointed legal guardian. In most cases, the insurer settled for a release signed by a minor, though not without misgivings. "We cannot help feeling some apprehension as a boy 15 years old . . . is not bound by his release if he chooses to back out; however we will hope for the best" (ML30, 5/4/97).

When the presumption of liability was strong, however, a "friendly" suit against the employer on behalf of the injured "infant" worker was arranged by the insurer to forestall later claims. Whether such arrangements were legal and ethical hinged upon whether all concerned fully understood the purpose of the procedure. It is doubtful that consent would have been given by even the most unsophisticated person if it were explained that the object of the sham law suit was to avoid the contingency of having to pay more later.

In the case of Isabella Salmon, when the insurer feared a large judgment (on the basis of having paid $300 and doctor's bills under similar circumstances three years earlier in another case), a suit was filed against the Dwight Manufacturing Company *on behalf of the young woman by an attorney recommended by the insurance company.* A prearranged judgment for doctor bills, four weeks' wages and $100 was entered when the suit was filed, thus closing the case. The insurer advised the mill agent: "You will therefore please employ Mr. Luther White or some other reputable attorney in Chicopee to bring friendly suit against you for the purpose of making a binding settlement. . . . Mr. White will understand this" (ML33, 7/19/00). The probability is great that the attorney for the plaintiff had an understanding with the defendant's insurer involving conflict of interest. There is a strong suspicion of fraud, in the absence of informed consent by the victim, and at the very least, there was an attempt to shortcut proper legal procedures.

The understanding between this particular attorney and the employer emerges in subsequent correspondence. A letter from the private secretary of the Governor of Massachusetts reveals an attempt by the mill management to influence a judicial appointment. "I am directed by His Excellency the Governor to acknowledge receipt of your letter of the 21st instant, and to say in reply that your recommendation of Mr. Luther White for appointment as Justice of the Chicopee Police Court will have his careful consideration" (ML35, 9/22/03). The success of this attempt to place a servant of the corporation on the bench of justice is documented by a letter from Luther White to the mill agent. It reveals the sort of relationship that impugns the impartiality of a court: "I am sorry to say that this will be my last bill for retainer. I do not consider it will be proper for me to take a retainer while I hold a court—even a minor court, but I will be glad to serve you whenever I can and you will save the retainer" (ML36, 1/14/04). Just what sort of service this newly appointed police court judge was promising to render free of charge to his patron is unspecified. One might suppose that strikers and others in conflict with management received short shrift before that bench.

The legal counsel retained by the impoverished casualties may have been tempted to ingratiate themselves with the adversary of their clients. This double-dealing is suggested by a letter from the attorney representing a man who lost a finger in a Dwight Manufacturing Company carding machine: "As is my custom I will not bring any action on this claim until I hear from you if within a reasonable time and not then if I am convinced there is not a good case for negligence against your company" (ML37, 11/22/05). From the tone of this communication it is not unreasonable to infer a claim for respectability from a lawyer who is saying "look how reasonable and responsible I am." The interests of the client may have been sacrificed by attorneys seeking to shake off the stigma attached to so-called ambulance chasing, or personal injury practice.[5]

Two volumes in a clerk's neat hand setting forth narrative accounts of work injuries at the Hamilton Manufacturing Company in Lowell have been preserved. They chronicle in the most lurid detail the suffering and pain of the mill casualties and indicate how frequently the deprivation was compounded by blaming the victim.

Angie Eaton, about 30 years of age, employed on the third floor of No 6 weaving room was injured . . . by accidentally slipping and sitting down violently upon an oil can which she had placed on the window sill a few moments before. The tube of the oil can penetrated her private parts and ruptured an artery, causing considerable loss of blood. We cannot yet determine the full extent of the injury. The injury was caused by her own carelessness as she should not have placed the oil can upon the window sill. She was taken to her home in a carriage and a physician summoned.[6]

The imputation of carelessness in this case, used to set up the defense against charges of negligence under the Employers' Liability Law, epitomizes management's callous attitude toward the victim. The accident itself, one of numerous injuries caused by sharp metal objects, broken glass, and falling objects, is evidence of the poor state of industrial housekeeping at that time. Surely there is no reason to suppose that workers then were inherently more clumsy than now. Safety campaigns, improved first aid, and medical assistance, as well as stiffer penalties (from insurers and the state) for poor housekeeping procedures are more likely explanations of improvements in this area than a decline of clumsiness.

Earlier in 1890, Albert Beckwith, aged fifteen, had been caught in the mechanism of a mule spinning machine that he was cleaning and suffered a severe abdominal wound. "No one was at fault except the boy, as he should have used more care," wrote the clerk, adding that the victim was taken to the hospital "as he had no friends" (Vol. 113, 1/2/90).

Another young worker, fourteen-year-old Virginia Rancour, while engaged in her work, suffered bruised fingers and a cut described as not serious. Though it was a minor injury, the case demonstrates the employer's senseless response. The report stated: "The girl cannot give a clear explanation of just how the accident occurred as she does not understand our language, but it was evidently the result of extreme carelessness on her part" (Vol. 113, 5/6/91). Immigrant labor was perceived to be in limitless supply and therefore, presumably expendable. Inability to understand English was no excuse for workers when employers leveled accusations of contributory negligence, although in cases of litigation, interpreters were produced to testify that the foreign-born workers had received job instructions in their native language.

The narrative injury reports are replete with expressions of an accusatory rhetoric whose undoubted object was the establishment of a defense of contributory negligence. Over and over the records echo with phrases such as: no one but himself is to blame, the boy's own carelessness, she is wholly to blame, or if he had used more caution it would not have happened.

A common admonition was that a worker had been told repeatedly to keep away from the gears. Failure to keep away from a gear is given as evidence of contributory negligence in a case report in 1895, eighteen years after the enactment of legislation requiring that gears be covered. The report refers to a girl who was only fourteen years old when she lost part of one of her fingers (Vol. 112, 6/12/95).

In some cases, when the victim could not plausibly be blamed for his or her own injury, a fellow servant was held responsible. In one of the Hamilton cases, a loom fixer lost a portion of one of his fingers. He was repairing a loom "and while engaged in the work the girl tending the loom started it and . . . cut off the end of his left index finger." In another case, a weaver suffered a hand injury when his wife started the machine. "His wife is to blame for the accident, as she was meddling with something that was none of her business" (Vol. 113,

4/18/90; 2/12/92). Workers had little recourse in instances like these.

Unsafe material-handling practices could have grave consequence for the hapless employee who happened to be in the wrong place at the wrong time, as is seen in the case of A. C. Moody.

[He] was unloading acid from a truck this P.M. and finding one of the carboys broken he pulled it off the truck onto the ground, which caused the acid to spatter up into his face, which was somewhat burned and his right eye destroyed. . . . The accident was due to his own carelessness as he should have got assistance in handling the carboy and should have heeded Mr. Gardner, who, seeing what he was about to do, shouted to him not to unload it without help. [Vol. 113, 4/15/91]

Power transmission from a central source and the frequent absence or inadequacy of protective guards brought many mill workers to grief. In some cases the injuries were fatal, or, as happened to Michael Finnegan, resulted in seemingly minor cuts and abrasions and a narrow escape. "Michael Finnegan . . . got his clothes caught in the driving shaft of the machine, and was thrown around the shaft this P.M. His face was cut and arm and thigh chafed, and he was sent to the Hospital. Accident due to his own carelessness" (Vol. 112, 6/28/95).

The accident reports and correspondence from the liability insurer to the Lawrence Manufacturing Company in Lowell also present a bleak picture. The treatment of labor as an expendable factor of production is epitomized by the experience of Charles John, a twenty-eight-year-old Armenian whose arm was caught in the gears of a machine on October 26, 1892. The arm was badly crushed, and amputation just below the shoulder was performed at Lowell Hospital. In assessing blame, the injury report stated: "There were no witnesses to the accident, but he had no occasion to put his arm near the gears, as the machine was in good working order, and it must have been the result of his own carelessness. He had been cautioned by the overseer, with the aid of an interpreter in regard to the dangerous parts of the machine and instructed not to clean the gears or other parts of the machine while in motion."

Two weeks after the accident, John's overseer went to the hospital with an interpreter to visit the injured man. In a letter to the Lawrence Company treasurer, the mill agent reported:

Mr. McDavitt said that when he entered the room the man appeared to be quiet, but as soon as he saw them he commenced to groan, and kept it up all the time they were in the room. . . . Mr. McDavitt asked him, supposing that he (McDavitt) could raise money enough to take him home to Armenia, if he would like to go, to which he replied that he would not, as he couldn't do anything after he got there, he said he got 25 cents a day in Armenia and $1.00 a day here. . . . Mr. McDavitt asked him if he didn't think there was something he could do in his room, after he got round again, if he didn't think he could run an elevator, or something of that kind. John replied that he didn't know and . . . that he didn't want to have any talk with him about it. As it was very hard to get anything out of him, or to get him to say anything about his future plans . . . the inference is that he has been coached by someone.[7]

The idea that a man who lost his arm should be offered a ticket to go back to Armenia seems to imply not only that the disabled were relegated to the scrap heap, but that since this scrap heap was unsightly and troublesome it should be as far away as possible.

In the adversary process over injury costs the involvement of informers was not uncommon. One such case was documented in the Lawrence Manufacturing Company papers by a letter from the mill agent to the company treasurer:

One John McManus . . . says that he is possessed of certain information relative to the suit of Isaac Marchand the painter who was injured by falling from a staging . . . which would be of value to us. He asserts that Marchand, in conjunction with a certain French doctor, is endeavoring to exaggerate the injuries sustained . . . by making an account of medical attendance and visits far beyond the point for which there was any necessity. This McManus was formerly employed in our pipe shop and was discharged, and his object is undoubtedly to secure either a job, or some pecuniary compensation for himself. While information obtained from such a source may not be very reliable, yet I advise you in the matter . . . [GO1, 7/10/91]

This kind of maneuvering was a by-product of the adversary process over the costs of work injuries. As in many other conflict situations, spies and informers trade in fact or fiction as third parties for the principals. Since they are most likely to serve those who can reward them best, we would expect them to offer their services to the employers rather than to the casualties.

An insight into conjugal relations emerges from the injury of Albina Richards, a hose mender who worked at the Lawrence Manufacturing Company for six dollars per week. In November 1902, she was hit on the head when a pipefitter working above her work area dropped a piece of pipe. Shortly after the accident, her husband signed a release, agreeing to settle the case for $25. She was forty-two years old, and yet her husband was not only asked to decide this matter on her behalf, but consented to do so. "A call was made on her husband who signed a release, expressing satisfaction with this adjustment. However, upon approaching the injured person after securing the husband's release, it seems that she refuses at the present time to sign a release" (GO4, 11/17/02; GP1, 12/13/02).

This proved to be a prudent action on her part, because about three weeks later she received a better offer and signed a release for $100 and payment of $1.25 for her hospital bill. The inference may be drawn that the employer sought out the injured worker's husband in the expectation that she was a sufficiently subservient wife to accept a low settlement in deference to her spouse.

In June 1891, Isaac Charretier lost his right eye when a feed belt broke on a machine he was tending, and he was struck in the eye, probably by a belt hook. Three weeks after the injury, the mill agent sent a letter to the company treasurer.

Dr. Mignault has been here again this morning with Isaac Charretier . . . and says that Charretier has concluded to come down in his demands to Three Thousand Dollars, which Mignault thinks is the bottom figure. . . . He also talks about the other eye being endangered by the loss of this one for which there is no apparent ground. . . . [Given] the present attitude of these people . . . I can do nothing more with them. [GO1, 6/19/91]

Two aspects of this case are worth noting. The first is that the physician appeared as an agent of the patient rather than of the employer, a situation that the corporations and their insurers sought to avoid whenever possible. The second is the apparent willingness of a layman in management to second-guess the victim's physician, something which was generally unnecessary if the company doctor retained control of a case. In this adversary process the stakes were not "an eye for an eye," but an eye for the least amount of money from the insurer that the victim would accept.

Impugning the character of the plaintiff in injury cases was another tactic employed to avoid payment of damages. In forwarding to the treasurer a summons served on behalf of a worker who claimed she had been injured when a wall collapsed in one of the Lawrence mills, the agent wrote, "She is an old woman, and we find that her record is bad, she having been arrested several times for drunkeness" (GO2, 4/9/96). The intent was undoubtedly to discredit the complaining witness.

In another situation involving a fourteen-year-old boy who lost an arm, the boy's own attorney called the victim's intelligence into question, apparently to underscore the culpability of the employer in exposing a minor who was not very bright to the hazards of unguarded machinery. "The said Telesphore Butcher is not, and was not at the time a boy up to the standard of intelligence of boys of his age. . . . No interpreter was brought to him to show him how to do his work with safety. . . . while working as best he knew how and in the exercise of due care his hand got caught between the steel rolls of a winder . . . and his hand and arm were destroyed" (GO2, 1/27/93).

The agent was worried that his witnesses against Butcher might abscond. "The interpreter who communicated the instructions . . . is one Napoleon Bonneau, and the only witness to the accident that we can find is one Leon Stone. . . . In as much as these Frenchmen have a happy faculty of getting out of the way by running off to Canada to get rid of testifying, I submit the question whether it would not be wise to take these men's deposition in advance of a trial" (GO2, 1/30/93).

On April 6, 1900, there was a fire in one of the dust chimneys of the number ten mill at Lawrence. Remi Cote, a yard laborer, entered the burning structure and was struck on the head by a plank thrown down by another employee who was working above. Cote's neck was broken, and he was pronounced dead on arrival at the hospital. The injury report blamed the fatality on the victim, asserting that he "should not have stepped into the chimney, knowing that Matte was throwing down anything that was burning." The widow's law suit made a contrary claim, namely, that the death was a result of "the carelessness of [the mill] superintendent. A year later, the insurer paid $2,865 to settle the suit, of which $545 was allocated for legal fees" (GO3, 4/6/oo). That the court gave little credence to the defense of contributory negligence in this case can be inferred from the judgment awarded to Cote's heirs, which was large by the standards of 1900.

After losing his right arm in a carding machine on July 30, 1902, Michael Barras died within twenty minutes of his admission to the hospital. The mill agent wrote to the company treasurer: "A brother of the man who was killed here last week came to see if we could do anything for his wife and children and I told him that I did not see how we could. Do you wish this decision to stand?" A suit was filed by a Boston attorney, stating that the deceased, while employed in the carding room and "in the exercise of due care . . . received great bodily injury from which he languished and died, and for which I claim damages." A court order was issued attaching corporate assets to the value of $20,000. The summons warned the management: "Fail not of appearance at your peril." The threat to the employer was not terribly effective, and typically, the cause of the injured worker was thwarted. On September 23, 1903 the liability insurer reported that the case had been settled for $460" (GO4, 7/30/02; 8/4/02; 10/24/02).

The Lowell Hospital register for 1899–1905 traces the fate of some of the mill casualties listed in company records. During the period covered by the hospital document, there were 348 injury reports in the Lawrence Manufacturing Company Collection. Of these, 261 (72.9 percent) involved the hospital, including 229 (87.7 percent) who were treated in the outpatient department, 1 who was dead on arrival, and 31 (11.9 percent) who were admitted as bed patients. The duration of hospitalization ranged from one day for Louis Vallos, who died within twenty minutes of his admission after his right arm was torn from his body in a carding machine accident, to 104 days in the case of Sam Dyko, who thigh was scalded in a dye house spillage and required skin grafts.[8]

The average length of hospitalization was 24.3 days. For lacerations and open wounds the average was 25.6 days (compared with a 1972 United States average of 5.3 days) and for fractures, 25.4 days (compared with a 1972 United States average of 11.5 days for all ages and 9.0 days for patients aged 15–44). The average cost of hospitalization for the 31 Lawrence employees was $9.41 with an average weekly cost of $2.58. Table 14 illus-

TABLE 13. *Lawrence Manufacturing Company Injuries, 1899–1905*

Type of Care		Number	Percentage
Hospital Cases		261	75.0
Outpatient treatments	229		
Admitted as bed patients	31		
Dead on arrival	1		
Visited family physician		10	2.9
Went home		60	17.2
Remained at work		17	4.9
TOTAL		348	100.0

SOURCE: Lowell Hospital Register, 9/24/99 to 11/10/05, in St. Joseph's Hospital, Lowell, Mass., and Lawrence Manufacturing Company Collection, vol. GO3 and GO4, in Baker Library, Harvard University, Cambridge, Mass.

TABLE 14. *Casualties Admitted to Lowell Hospital from Lawrence Manufacturing Company, 1899–1905*

Age	Sex	Weekly Wage	Hospital Days	Hospital Cost	Cause	Case Description
15	M	$ 3.94	27	$10.61	machinery	scalp wound, lost part of ear
21	M	6.37	38	14.93	machinery	severed hand tendons
41	M	7.00	66	25.93	falling object	fractured leg
30	M	6.00	26	10.61	machinery	amputated finger
38	M	7.00	85	33.39	machinery	2 fingers amputated from each hand
40	M	9.86	2	.78	machinery	2 fingers amputated
28	M	11.50	2	.78	machinery	amputated finger
35	M	7.00	10	2.75	machinery	amputated finger
52	M	7.00	13	5.11	machinery	lacerated hands
42	M	7.00	12	4.71	machinery	fractured fingers, 1 amputated
16	F	4.90	19	4.75	machinery	fractured finger
19	M	2.94	6	2.36	sat on shears	punctured scrotum
56	M	9.80	16	6.28	fall	injured side
21	F	4.90	13	3.25	machinery	amputated finger
35	M	4.90	1	.39	machinery	severed arm; died 20 min. after admission
60	M	5.50	6	2.36	fall	sprained back
42	F	6.00	5	1.25	falling object	head wound
36	M	6.64	13	5.11	machinery	severed arm
17	F	4.90	8	2.00	machinery	fractured finger
45	M	6.64	7	2.75	fall	injured side
33	M	7.00	22	8.64	machinery	amputated arm
33	F	7.00	10	3.57	machinery	fractured fingers
63	M	8.70	12	4.71	machinery	lacerated hand; died from infection
25	M	7.00	17	6.68	elevator	crushed toe
25	M	7.00	13	5.11	splinter	infected foot
45	M	6.64	104	44.78	dye spill	scalded thigh; skin graft
26	M	7.00	43	16.89	machinery	3 fingers amputated
52	M	10.84	10	3.93	fall	fractured arm
21	F	4.50	8	2.34	falling object	knee injury
25	M	7.00	78	30.64	machinery	lacerated hand
22	M	6.64	62	24.36	machinery	fractured hand, 4 fingers amputated

SOURCE: Register of Lowell Hospital, 1899–1905 in St. Joseph's Hospital, Lowell, Mass.; Lawrence Manufacturing Company collection, vols. GO3 and GO4, Baker Library, Harvard University, Cambridge, Mass.

trates the hospital experience of some of the mill workers injured in Lowell around the turn of the twentieth century.

Of the 31 Lawrence workers hospitalized between 1899 and 1905, 30 (96.8 percent) were foreign-born, including 12 Greeks, 12 French Canadians, 2 British, and 4 of other nationalities. Though women comprised about 60 percent of the labor force, only 6 (19.4 percent) of the hospital patients were women. The most dangerous jobs were in the carding rooms, which were responsible for 41.9 percent of the injuries. Cause of the injuries was distributed as follows: machinery, 20; falls, 4; falling objects, 3; and miscellaneous, 4.

In the process of apportioning the costs of work injuries, the interplay of adversaries and the intervention of third parties served to place the greatest burden on those who could least afford it, namely, the injured employees themselves. In a social context more conducive to the maintenance of property interests than to humane concerns, for every Bridget Linehan who stood her ground to collect in full, there were scores of Victoria Guyettes who *were* beaten down. In short, the Chicopee method was a form of exploitation. Employers applied and workers resisted the Chicopee method, creating one of the antagonisms of industrial conflict.

Under the Employers' Liability Law the conflict over work hazards was waged with far greater intensity on the employers' side than on the side of the casualties. That asymmetry, unarguably documented in the case records that have been preserved, may be attributed to the provenance of the law and to the social fragmentation of the labor force. The law originated in judge-made common law, as well as in legislation that did not reflect the working class interests. The lack of worker solidarity was a result of ethnic diversity, as well as the social and geographic mobility of the labor force. Despite the catalog of horror tales from an earlier industrial age, there is a positive element, that is, that the rule of law is preferable to arbitrary and unrestricted exercise of power. The Employers' Liability Laws—unjust as they were from the perspective of injured workers—over time created such constraints and uncertainties on employers that important elements of the dominant class came to view them as counterproductive and supported social insurance legislation that dispensed with assessment of negligence. Reforms in the "law of the killed and wounded" along with other important legislation in the six decades after 1910 have changed the groundrules for conflict over work hazards in the United States.

CHAPTER 5

Six Decades of Reform

IN THE six decades after 1910, numerous important reform measures contributed to the amelioration of American workers' lives. This liberalization of society reflects the interplay of complex forces. Among these forces was the consolidation of citizenship rights and the utilization of those rights by workers to influence legislation. Another was a realization by privileged groups that enactment of reforms would forestall more radical challenges to the existing order. Technological development made it possible for productivity to rise and for real income to increase over long periods, providing amelioration without significant redistribution. Exploitive relations with underdeveloped countries also contributed to improved levels of living in the developed ones.

The three major reforms affecting work hazards and industrial conflict were the Workmen's Compensation Acts passed in all states between 1911 and 1948; the National Labor Relations Act of 1935 (Wagner Act), which legitimized unionization and collective bargaining; and the Occupational Safety and Health Act of 1970. Each of these reforms has contributed substantially to changing the institutional framework in which industrial conflict takes place. The underlying class inequalities in risk of injury or occupational illness remain largely unchanged, as does the employers' motive to minimize costs related to safety and health, but the ground rules governing the conflict have changed dramatically, mitigating the disadvantages under which manual workers labor.

NO-FAULT SOCIAL INSURANCE

The fate of industrial casualties under employers' liability has been documented above. A laissez-faire ideology and a perception of the labor supply as limitless and expendable contributed to an industrial climate in which it could be asserted that "many employers . . . regard safety work as a 'socialistic fad' and effective compulsion is exercised in but a few states."[1] The need to convince juries that work injuries and occupational disease cases were entirely the fault of the employer—without the extenuating circumstance of contributory negligence, assumption of risk, or negligence on the part of a fellow servant—was a barrier against effective compulsion in the realm of occupational safety and health. Thus, a principle of strict liability, that is liability irrespective of fault, came to be favored by many because the assessment of negligence had become hopelessly entangled in the complexities of industrial organization and machine technology. Moreover, the premise of freedom and equality of the parties to a labor contract upon which tort law rested had become an anachronism in "a society in which more and more vicissitudes threaten a multitude of individuals whose liberty to avoid them shrinks steadily."[2]

An alternative model existed in Germany, where compulsory workmen's compensation had been passed in 1884, and another in Britain, where Parliament passed a compensation act in 1897. American jurisdictions lagged behind the European examples; a 1902 Maryland workmen's compensation law was struck down as unconstitutional. The first real workmen's compensation law in the United States, although quite limited in scope, was passed by Congress in 1908 to cover certain federal employees. Between 1910 and 1920, forty-two states passed compensation laws, and the last of the states to do so, Mississippi, enacted a statute in 1948. The objective of these laws, which vary greatly from state to state, is to cover part of the wages lost by victims of injury or disease arising out of, and in the course of, employment, and to defray the cost of medical care and rehabilitation services, without regard in most instances, to any determination of negligence.

The sequence of events in the field of workmen's compensation did not stop in 1948, when the last state enacted such a law, but continued in an ongoing process. The level of benefits paid, the occupational diseases that are covered, and the presently excluded categories of employees to be brought under the protection of compensation laws are areas of continuing concern. The availability and quality of treatment and rehabilitation programs in each jurisdiction are other issues. The progression of these concerns will be traced in this chapter, describing the origin of compensation programs and the way in which they superseded employers' liability.

While social reform groups like the American League for Labor Legislation denounced the inequities of employers' liability and advocated change to a no-fault system, support from business interests promoted the emergence of workmen's compensation. In 1910 the head of the National Association of Manufacturers said: "The spirit of the times is leading toward a visionary conception of life and duty, and . . . the atmosphere is charged with the murmurings of discontent, upon which the agitator fattens and the political demagogue thrives." For these reasons, he argued, business interests should support workmen's compensation, but on their own terms, namely, "the most conservative and least expensive scheme." Rubinow observed in 1913 that "the effort to make compensation cheap rather than just was very prominent" in employer-supported legislation, whose sponsors "flatly stated their preference for compensation provided it did not cost any more than the . . . wasteful liability system."[3] This view is corroborated by Roy Lubove who suggests that "business imperatives proved more influential in shaping workmen's compensation than considerations of equity or social expediency."[4]

In contrast to the support of corporate interests and social insurance reformers during the early stages of the movement, labor unions reacted coolly to the proposed change. Labor opposition to workmen's compensation was based "on the belief that a weakening of the employer's traditional defenses would produce many court victories and high awards from sympathetic juries."[5] Unions wished to retain employers' liability laws, stripped of the loopholes used to defeat workers' claims.

Though workmen's compensation was "a radical departure from established practice," wrote Asher, "it was supported by economic groups usually considered conservative."[6] One of the corporate goals in sponsoring this type of legislation was to undercut unionists and other advocates of an adversary posture in industrial relations. A steel corporation executive expressed the hope that "the progress of workmen's compensation should be a rebuke and a rebuttal to those who assert that working-men get nothing except by contest and struggle."[7]

After 1905, when industrial injuries reached their peak and the safety movement called attention to this national scandal, juries tended to become more sympathetic to plaintiffs in work injury suits. "This trend in tort litigation, resulting as employers saw it, from 'those damnable suits brought by the shyster lawyers,' made employers feel that the courts were trying to 'down us.'"[8] Fear that such a trend would continue encouraged employer support for compensation laws. On the worker side this trend in litigation motivated union efforts to "continue and strengthen employer's liability as well, giving the employee a choice of remedy,"[9] to avoid having to give up the substantial damages awarded by sympathetic juries in some cases.

Notwithstanding the decisive support for workmen's compensation by interest groups like the National Association of Manufacturers, there was last-ditch opposition to changing the liability law. The first New York workmen's compensation act was declared unconstitutional in the 1911 state supreme court decision of *Ives* v. *South Buffalo Railway Co.*[10] The judges argued that imposition of strict liability on employers irrespective of fault would deprive them of property without due process; that the classification of dangerous employments in the state law being struck down violated the equal protection clause of the Fourteenth Amendment; that the right to a trial by jury was abrogated by procedural sections of the law; and that the defenses of the common law could not be eliminated by the legislature.

The reaction to this decision was critical. "It is not that our judges are corrupt," observed Theodore Roosevelt, "but that they are absolutely reactionary, and their decisions . . . have been such as almost to bar the path to industrial, economic and social reform. By such decisions they add immensely to the strength of the Socialist Party, they perpetuate misery, they increase unrest and discontent."[11] Later a legal scholar commented on judicial attempts to stem the reform movement: "The assumption of risk is purely the judicial invention of Lord Abinger, Chief Justice Shaw and Baron Alderson. Yet so powerfully do legal fictions work and so short is the legal memory of men, that a doctrine of which there was no trace before 1837 is in 1911 treated as a law of nature, and courts doubt whether a legislature has the right to abolish it."[12]

Workmen's compensation, in barring suits by injured employees, "is in the nature of a compromise, by which the workman is to accept a limited compensation, usually less than the estimate which a jury might place upon his damages, in return for an extended liability of the employer, and an assurance that he will be paid."[13] The outcome of the compromise reflects the asymmetry of power between the contending groups, and while there have been ongoing attempts to introduce no-fault insurance into other fields of personal injury litigation, "the compromise which the occupationally injured made for the innovation of this principle remains fixed and progressively more disadvantageous to them."[14] In a number of instances, labor union officials advocated removal of the common law defenses that impeded remedies under the employers' liability laws and strongly objected to the provision of American compensation laws that barred the alternative of litigation for negligence. The subsequent characterization of the compromise as disadvantageous to injured workers attests to the foresight of these union officials. However, since the elimination of injury litigation was one of the motives of the powerful business interests that supported the compensation laws, there probably never was much chance for passage of compensation laws that retained the option to litigate. Another shortcoming of the early compensation laws was that none that was passed before 1914 included provisions for occupational disease.

It is debatable whether, in fact, workmen's compensation was a "radical departure" in labor legislation. "The injured worker, rather than the employer or industry, continued to bear most of the costs," according to Lubove, who went on to say that the program "never overcame its structural deficiencies, rooted in benefit schedules adapted more to business imperatives than to the objective needs of injured workers."[15] Nominal benefits under workmen's compensation are from one-half to two-thirds of the injured worker's lost pay, but in practice the level of compensation is from one-fourth to one-third—to say nothing of workers' having to bear 100 percent of the attendant pain and suffering. A further disadvantage exists in the imposition of a waiting period during which nothing is paid. The lag time between injury and compensation reduces benefits in temporary disability cases. Workers are hindered by the arbitrary ceilings on the number of weeks that benefits continue, which means that only temporary aid is provided for permanent disability.[16]

Somers and Somers discuss the current disdain among workers toward workmen's compensation, as illustrated by the advice given to apprentice printers: "If you are going to mangle a hand, don't do it on the job. You get twice as much if it's not on workmen's compensation." The same authors point out that as "a percentage of payroll, net costs [of workmen's compensation] have remained fairly constant since the middle thirties, averaging about 1 per cent."[17]

Opponents of social insurance for work injuries argued, like Walter Nichols, that under the spirit of the U.S. Constitution, employers could not be made liable for injuries for which they were not at fault, and that imposition of such strict liability would be "an attack on the manhood of employees as American citizens." Such legislation could not be countenanced "unless our whole theory of government is to be abandoned for another on essentially socialistic lines."[18]

Workmen's compensation, in this view, which was held primarily by advocates of laissez faire and "rugged individualism," would degrade the workers covered under its provisions:

They are to be dealt with as incompetent wards of the state who must be protected against themselves, incapable of freely contracting for their services and subject like medieval serfs to assumed task-masters, who must answer for their safety and be responsible for their mishaps. . . . Politically, America knows no servile class. Is all this to be changed and a spirit of state socialism to be inculcated in our rising generation through the operation of laws which make the employer the keeper of those whom he employs?[19]

The fears of early opponents of no-fault social insurance in the field of work hazards—fears that the survival of the fit would be undermined and that state socialism would ensue—proved to be greatly exaggerated. On the other hand, although no scheme of workmen's compensation has ever lived up to its full potential—and never approached the socialistic dimensions that were feared by some—workers did benefit significantly. Under the former employers' liability laws, over 85 percent of the work-related casualties received nothing for their injuries.[20] The probability has increased that workers will receive partial recovery of damages in the form of income maintenance, medical care, and/or payment under dismemberment schedules. It is also much more likely that families will be awarded death benefits in the case of job-related deaths. Clearly there have been steps forward. However, if the intention of the reform was to eliminate the adversary conflicts surrounding work hazards and resulting casualties, that goal has proved to be elusive. Instead, workmen's compensation has changed the terms on which this conflict is waged, but has not displaced it with a harmonious order.

In a 1978 article entitled "Litigation-Prone Society," William J. McGill, president of Columbia University, complained about appearing as a defendant in thirty-five law suits. His explanation of this plight was that "after World War II our society began moving toward an adversary structure patterned on the model set down by labor law in the 1930's. In this structure, narrowly based constituencies each pressing for its own interest . . . clash against one another."[21] He implied that this plurality of interest groups should eschew the adversary process out of deference to national interest or public good. He was wrong if he supposed that suppression or subordination of divergent interests would be a step forward, but he provided an acute insight by alluding to New Deal labor legislation as an important institutional foundation for the right of subordinated or disadvantaged groups to challenge more powerful or privileged ones.

Legal protection of union membership antedated the New Deal period, not only in the Norris-LaGuardia Act, but in earlier measures, some dating from World War I years. However, the present institutional pattern of union rights and collective bargaining ground rules originated in the National Industrial Recovery Act. This law was a patchwork measure intended to cover a number of contingencies of the Great Depression, and it provided for the relaxation of antitrust laws to accommodate production codes and price regulation; public-sector employment through works projects; and, in response to pressure from unions, a stipulation that workers had a right to bargain collectively through unions of their choice.[22] Section 7(a) of the National Industrial Recovery Act provided that "employees shall have the right to organize and bargain collectively through representatives of their own choosing, and shall be free from interference, restraint or coercion of employers of labor, or their agents, in the designation of such representatives or in self-organization or in other concerted activities for the purpose of collective bargaining or other mutual protection."[23]

In a court case in 1935 that tested Section 7(a), the Federal District Court in Delaware sustained Weirton Steel Company's refusal to permit a bargaining election among its employees. The court rejected as "revolutionary" the federal government's contention that union organization must be given the protection of law in order to redress the disparity of power between employer and employee. This contention, according to the court, was "based on the assumption of an inevitable and necessary diversity of interests. This is the traditional old world theory. It is not the Twentieth Century American theory of that relation as dependent upon mutual interest, understanding and good will."[24] The supposedly "traditional old world theory" was epitomized in 1787 by James Madison in Federalist No. 10, while what the judge referred to as the "Twentieth Century American theory" was already a long-established belief when John of Salisbury, Bishop of Chartres, elaborated it in the twelfth century.[25] Madison perceived that "division of society into different interests and parties" was inherent in human nature. "Liberty is to faction what air is to fire," he argued, and elimination of factional interests would entail destruction of liberty. That being undesirable, he proposed means for controlling the effects of faction by limiting the mischief that can be done by the more powerful to the less. By contrast, John of Salisbury made the subordination of the "feet" to the "head" absolute in his body metaphor, evoked as a twentieth century American theory in *United States* v. *Weirton Steel Company.*

By establishing a right for workers to organize unions and a duty for employers to bargain in good faith, the Congress put into practice a Madisonian principle of balancing factions whereby the position of organized workers becomes less onerous than it was under open-shop conditions. The legislation also provided a framework of recognition and organization conducive to abatement of the intensity and violence of the conflict.[26]

Though there was substantial growth in bona fide labor unions under the National Industrial Recovery Act, the "major result of Section 7(a) appears to have been the rise of [employer-dominated] company unions," which doubled in membership between 1932 and 1935.[27] Relying on what President Roosevelt denounced as a horse-and-buggy view of interstate commerce, the Supreme Court in 1935 struck down the National Industrial Recovery Act (NIRA) as unconstitutional.

New legislation was drafted that incorporated not only the basic provisions of Section 7(a), but which stipulated certain acts by employers to be unfair labor practices subject to cease and desist orders of an administrative agency, the National Labor Relations Board (NLRB). This law, the National Labor Relations Act of 1935 (Wagner Act), along with other legislation, faced a fate in the Supreme Court similar to that of the NIRA. This prospect prompted President Roosevelt, early in his second term, to embark on his ill-fated court-packing maneuver designed to enlarge the high court and to create vacancies that would be filled with justices more willing to uphold his program. Though Roosevelt's plan apparently was doomed to failure, whatever support for its adoption that existed was dissipated when Justice Owen Roberts changed his position and joined a five to four vote sustaining the constitutionality of the Wagner Act.

This law provided that employees "shall have the right to self-organization, to form, join or assist labor organizations, to bargain collectively through representatives of their own choosing, and to engage in concerted activities, for the purposes of collective bargaining or other mutual aid or protection." This right was buttressed by five newly-proscribed unfair labor practices: (1) to interfere with, restrain, or coerce employees in the exercise of the rights guaranteed in section 7; (2) to dominate or interfere with the formation or administration of any labor organization; (3) by discrimination in regard to hire or tenure of employment or any term or condition of employment to encourage or discourage membership in any labor organization; (4) to discharge or otherwise discriminate against an employee because he has filed charges or given testimony under this Act; and (5) to refuse to bargain collectively with the representatives of his employees. Another section guaranteed that any individual employee or group of employees shall have the right at any time to present grievances to their employer.

Imposition on employers of a duty to bargain has been crucial. Protection of union organization without a corresponding obligation for employers to act in good faith to arrive at collective agreements would confer on workers a meaningless right. Ross argues that this law "played a fundamental role in the . . . development of collective bargaining." As an enduring piece of legislation, the Wagner Act serves to institutionalize collective bargaining because "the price of breaking a union has been raised;"[28] litigating unfair labor practice cases is often more costly than recognition of a union.

Along with other New Deal enactments, the Wagner Act was anathema to many retrograde interests, which began a campaign for its revision immediately after its passage. In the wake of the 1946 Congressional elections, these efforts achieved success with the passage of the Labor Management Relations Act of 1947. The Taft-Hartley Act, as it is generally called, was, according to Representative Powell, written by "over a score of corporation lawyers . . . paid by big business." President Truman, in his veto message, declared it to be "a clear threat to the successful working of our democratic society." The powerful alignment of forces on the side of management is revealed by the vote to override the presidential veto: 331 to 83 in the House and 68 to 25 in the Senate.[29] Though it placed restrictions on hitherto sanctioned activities of unions and lifted restrictions imposed earlier on employers, the new law left intact the rights of self-organization and concerted activities. Likewise, the unfair labor practices against which employers were enjoined under the Wagner Act, including the provision which imposes the duty to bargain, remained prohibited, and the right to present grievances was reaffirmed in the new labor law. Finally, while greatly restricting strikes and boycotts, there is a "saving provision," Section 502, which states: "Nothing in this Act shall be construed to require an individual employee to render labor or service without his consent . . . nor shall the quitting of labor by any employee or employees in good faith because of abnormally dangerous conditions for work at the place of employment . . . be deemed a strike under this Act." In the early years following its enactment, Section 502 was viewed as providing protection of concerted action by employees who refused to work under unusual hazards. Later court decisions, however, have resulted in a "substantial erosion . . . of Sec. 502 protection," because the subjective good faith of workers who walked off their jobs would no longer suffice in the absence of credible evidence of abnormally dangerous conditions. The weakening of this protection is unfortunate, but at the very least Section 502 indicates congressional recognition of a conflict situation and of the inadequacy of protracted negotiation about imminent danger.[30]

The significance of the Labor Management Relations Act for safety and health issues was affirmed by the NLRB in a 1966 decision declaring negotiation of safety rules to be a mandatory subject of collective bargaining. The Board, in *Gulf Power and L.U.'s 1055 and 624 IBEW*, declared that "safety provisions constitute an essential part of the employees' terms and conditions of employment, and, as such, are a mandatory subject of bargaining." The Board found no merit in Gulf Power's argument that "statutory provisions requiring that it exercise a high degree of care in its operations render all matters pertaining to safety a prerogative of management and therefore immune from bargaining."[31] Refusal to bargain on the issue of safety was declared to be an unfair labor practice from which the employer was ordered to cease and desist.

The Wagner Act and those of its provisions that survived the Eightieth Congress provided a fundamental reform of the context for the struggle over work hazards. By conferring legitimacy on unions and on collective bargaining, this legislation secured for manual workers rights of citizenship which previously had been far more precarious. The right to representation by a union and the right to present grievances meant that safety and health in the workplace became subject to the scrutiny of and amelioration by labor organizations in ways that had been inaccessible to unorganized workers. Moreover, since bona fide labor unions will negotiate production standards with the goal of mitigating speedup and stretchout, collective bargaining has an indirect effect on safety through abatement of two of the principal causes of injuries, pressure to increase production and the resulting fatigue. With respect to Workmen's Compensation, unions perform the important function of providing representation for workers in compensation cases. Unions also benefit workers through political action to broaden coverage. Finally, nurtured under the Wagner Act and able to survive, by and large, under the less benign aegis of Taft-Hartley, unions gained in political influence to help shape the Occupational Safety and Health Act (OSHA), which in turn enhanced union concern over work hazards.

OCCUPATIONAL SAFETY AND HEALTH ACT

Many years elapsed between the early proliferation of industrial hazards in America and the passage of the Occupational Safety and Health Act of 1970, the first comprehensive federal law to provide for the establishment and enforcement of safety and health standards. The pretext for this neglect was that the individual states were competent to deal with such matters. The only national legislation prior to OSHA was a poorly en-

forced law dealing with health and safety of government contract workers as well as isolated laws dealing with hazards
faced by miners, longshoremen, and atomic energy workers.
Aside from these scattered exceptions, the law establishing
OSHA was literally without precedent.

A bill along these lines was first introduced without success
by Hubert Humphrey in 1951, and over the decade that followed similar attempts were made by others to no avail. After
a 1958 industrial disaster, the Secretary of Labor declined a request for the drafting of legislation to provide mandatory safety
standards in the handling of hazardous materials and claimed
that "the problem did not warrant federal intervention."[32]

A steady rise in industrial casualties during the decade beginning in 1958 and the emergence of the environmentalist
movement in the 1960s contributed to belated congressional
action in this field. The rise in work casualties came to be recognized as a serious national problem. Environmentalists did
not need monumental powers of deduction to conclude that
industrial effluents causing air and water pollution had a corresponding impact on workers inside the workplace.

In 1968 President Johnson proposed comprehensive legislation to protect workers in their place of employment. The bill
that was drafted as the Occupational Safety and Health Act of
1968 failed to muster sufficient support for passage, despite the
compelling arguments marshalled in its support.

Labor Secretary Wirtz supported passage of the bill, citing
the need for uniform protection of workers irrespective of the
state in which they worked. As a result of leaving this function
of government to state agencies, Wirtz pointed out, there was
an inverse relationship between mortality rates from industrial
causes and state expenditures for promoting safety and health
in the workplace. "While we sit here talking this morning," he
told the Senate subcommittee before which he testified, "from
now until noon, 17 people in this country are going to be killed
while they are working on their jobs." He went on to cite sim-

ilarly grim statistics before noting the clash of interests at issue.

[The problem] isn't States' rights, although we all know that S.2864 is going to be opposed by those who confuse that principle with their own interest. . . . The issue . . . isn't cost. Although the issue is not the cost of protecting employees' safety and health, it will be opposed on that basis. . . . It is going to be a very fair question of those who oppose S.2864 on the basis of cost and expense to ask them just exactly what they regard as the price of a human life or a limb, or an eye, and whether they would regard the price the same for any family in America as they would for a member of their own family.[33]

Cost was and is the crucial underlying issue. The Secretary of Labor implicitly raised a question that is crucial to the analysis of class, to wit, that members of a privileged class will spare no expense in pursuit of their own and their families' safety and health, while at the same time avoiding costs of protecting the safety and health of members of another class. Such costs as they will bear for the life and limb of the servant or employee will be only those that are imposed by law. Because of the great variation among state laws in this area and the haphazard enforcement of most of them, Secretary Wirtz, Ralph Nader, and numerous other witnesses supported S.2864. The bill—"to assure safe and healthful working conditions for working men and women; to assist the States to participate in efforts to assure such working conditions; to provide for research, information, education and training in the field of occupational safety and health"—was never reported out of committee.[34]

The issue persisted, however, and the Ninety-First Congress proved to be receptive to proposals for legislating a federal presence in the area of workers' safety and health. Three bills were introduced and conflict over them raged until the end of 1970.

The points of contention were numerous. The administration wanted to create an independent board to set and enforce safety standards, but the Democratic bills vested these functions in the Department of Labor. Managerial interests supporting the former and labor unions the latter. Instead of seeking outright defeat of federal intervention (probably because passage of some sort of law was part of President Nixon's labor strategy), the corporate lobbyists sought to create a regulatory agency of the sort that has been so often co-opted by the interests it is supposed to regulate. The unions were vehemently opposed to this provision, and the corporations, no less vehemently, but less convincingly, objected to empowering the Department of Labor to serve this function on the grounds that the department was subservient to the unions.

There were disputes over the rights of employees to accompany government inspectors during the plant "walk-around" and over the authority of the Secretary of Labor to order plant closings in cases where imminent danger precluded time-consuming judicial processes.

The ebb and flow of confrontation and compromise in Congress, which produced the landmark OSHA legislation, replete with boycotts of committee meetings, parliamentary maneuvers to create a quorum to thwart the boycott, and a Republican filibuster in the Senate, have been chronicled elsewhere.[35] A decade after its enactment, the law and the programs it established continue as focal points of confrontation and compromise.

The effects of work hazards were declared to constitute a burden upon and hindrance to interstate commerce and a threat to the general welfare. Hence there was constitutional authority for Congress to enact legislation that sought to assure a safe and healthful work environment. The OSHA legislation imposed a general duty on employers to "furnish to each of his employees employment and a place of employment which are free from recognized hazards that are causing or are likely to cause death or serious physical harm to his employees . . . [and to] comply with occupational safety and health standards promulgated under this act."

OSHA established authority for the Secretary of Labor "to set mandatory occupational safety and health standards applicable to businesses affecting interstate commerce . . . provide research in the field of occupational safety and health . . . discover latent disease, establishing causal connections between diseases and work in environmental conditions." The training of occupational safety and health personnel was also provided for under the legislation.

The act prohibited giving employers advance notice of inspections and specified penalties both for violations of safety and health standards and for interference with investigators and inspectors employed by the Secretary of Labor under this law. The penalties specified include "imprisonment for any term of years or for life" for killing an inspector and for "assaulting or hampering the work of a Labor Department safety or health investigator or inspector," a fine up to $5,000 or up to three years in prison.

Labor unions played an important part in securing passage of the Occupational Safety and Health Act of 1970. In turn, the law has been, as Ashford writes, "important in providing a basis for union demands that basic safety and health standards be included in collective bargaining contracts. . . . Prior to the OSHA, collective bargaining did not adequately focus on or protect employee safety and health. Safety and health issues had low priority on the bargaining agenda and often were bartered for more pressing objectives."[36] Thus we see that there is a great deal of reciprocal influence among the laws considered in this chapter. The Wagner Act nurtured unionization and collective bargaining. The unions that gained strength under its aegis lobbied for OSHA, and the programs of OSHA raise the consciousness of union leaders concerning safety and health issues. The circle is completed by the provision in the Occupational Safety and Health Act for a commission to study state workmen's compensation laws to determine if such laws are adequate and to make recommendations for their improvement.

Far from eliminating industrial conflict, the laws discussed briefly in this chapter serve rather to direct the employer-worker adversary encounters over work hazards into newly created institutional channels. The clash of interests is inherent in the underlying class inequalities, but these reforms, so central to the liberalization of the system, have served to mitigate the effects of these inequalities. The final chapter will show some of the ways in which the ongoing conflict is shaped by these laws.

CHAPTER 6

Continuity and Change

THE concluding chapter discusses briefly how the patterns of the ongoing and unavoidable conflict over work hazards have been altered by the laws discussed in chapter 5. Workmen's Compensation, labor relations laws and the Occupational Safety and Health Act define three arenas in which industrial conflict over safety and health takes place.

Though some of the reformers in the early campaigns for no-fault coverage of industrial accidents may have been motivated by a desire for conflict abatement, their wish has not been realized. On the contrary, workmen's compensation laws have served to redefine some of the rules of a conflict that has increased rather than diminished. Workmen's Compensation was unarguably an advance over Employers' Liability Laws; a great majority of injured workers previously received nothing for their pains, while under workmen's compensation there is at least some payment in nearly all cases. In the realm of occupational disease the payment of compensation is still problematic in some states for some diseases, especially when employers dispute claims that a condition arose in and out of the course of employment. Formal adversary encounters are much more frequent under Workmen's Compensation than they had been under Employers' Liability, when insurers routinely and cheaply bought signed releases. Under Workmen's Compensation, conflict stems from "uncertainty as to whether an accident did or did not arise out of or in the course of employment" and over assessment of the extent of a claimant's disability.[1]

In 1954 Somers and Somers wrote that no national data existed on the proportion of workmen's compensation cases that were contested, but cited various estimates ranging from less than ten to thirty percent. They suggest that even if the actual proportion of contested workmen's compensation cases were known, "it would underestimate the importance of the contested cases, for they represent the more expensive cases involving the more serious injuries. Also, the decisions in contested cases tend to establish the criteria and standards which guide settlement in all cases."[2]

The dissemination of information on this topic had not improved by 1971, when the National Commission on State Workmen's Compensation Systems published data on contested cases as a percentage of all cases for the fifty states and had to report that no estimates were available for twenty-five of the states. In the other half of the states, 17 reported that fewer than 10 percent of compensation cases were contested, 3 states reported that 10 to 24.9 percent were contested, 5 states reported between 25 and 49.9 percent, and one state reported 50 percent or more.[3] "No matter how efficiently and properly a workmen's compensation system may operate," argued one authority, "it is inevitable that disputes will arise."[4]

If disputes are inherent even in the best possible compensation program, the sources of conflict in the present programs seem almost limitless. Physicians who sell expert testimony to either side, claimants' and employers' attorneys, union officials and insurance adjustors are among the third parties who benefit from fishing in the troubled waters of contested cases. Medical decisions are made which are adverse to the patients' interests on the advice of insurance carriers. Records are falsified while employers belittle injuries and claimants exaggerate.[5]

Legal fees in contested cases are also a focal point of conflict. In forty of fifty-six jurisdictions, the claimants have to pay the legal fees they incur. One staff report of the National Commission on State Workmen's Compensation Laws characterized this practice as one that forces the worker "to pay for the failures of the system." Benefits "are at a level which provides at best a minimal standard of living. Each dollar removed from the weekly benefit to pay for an attorney is a serious deprivation."[6]

One of the trade-offs forced on workers as a condition for no-fault workmen's compensation was the relinquishment of the right to sue for negligence in work injury cases. Some pro-labor people advocate restoring the right to a tort action as a supplementary remedy, along the lines of the British law on work injuries, since recoveries in negligence cases are often five to ten times greater than awards for comparable injuries in compensation cases.

Advocates of workmen's compensation had labored under the hope that relief would be automatic, that there would be less litigation and fewer opportunities for the enrichment of attorneys. This proved to be an unwarranted expectation, because uncertainties remained that delayed settlements, even though a much lower proportion of casualties were sent away empty-handed. Marcus points out that "the adversary element was inherent in the new system as it was in the old. And the chief result of the effort to eliminate lawyers, in the early years, was to eliminate lawyers on one side but not on the other." A legal specialty opposing compensation claims emerged that worked to the detriment of claimants. Under this one-sided adversary process, "instead of a claim for compensation being determined on grounds of public interest, it was opposed and obstructed at every stage by the adverse interest of the employer or his insurance company."[7]

After two decades of unilateral advocacy, a "plaintiff's bar" came into existence, appealing to lawyers who "were attracted to the idea of becoming defenders of the underdog," as well as to those who saw the rising volume of claims as a source of livelihood.[8] The adversary system, now less one-sided than in the early decades of workmen's compensation, is a necessary part of a program that embodies an ongoing divergence of interests between injured claimants and cost-conscious insurers.

Lawyers are not the only third parties drawn into the conflict created by the clash of divergent interests in the compensation system. Private detectives are often hired to discover whether compensation claimants are really disabled, or whether they are moonlighting on other jobs while collecting benefits. Other important third parties are the physicians on both sides of contested compensation cases, in which each side produces expert medical witnesses to support its arguments.

In a 1977 decision the Rhode Island workmen's compensation commissioner ruled that mental illness linked to job-related conditions can be compensable. Work-related stress incapacitated the claimant, according to testimony that led to the ruling. In the adversary proceedings before the commissioner, each side presented a psychiatrist as its expert witness. The claimaint's physician testified that the worker was "totally incapacitated from any gainful employment." The employer's psychiatrist admitted under cross-examination that there was "a reasonable medical probability" that she could have been disabled. In his decision, the commissioner conceded that there might be some question about his ability to "determine that a worker is not malingering when there is no actual physical injury to show that he had actually been hurt," and asserted that "each case of 'job stress' must be decided on the facts presented."[9]

Since illness and injury confer legitimacy on the nonfeasance of subordinates in many authority relationships, superiors perennially rely on medical experts to challenge claims of disability. Subordinates in turn have a compelling need for professionals to validate their claims. The interests of adversaries seeking to belittle, document, or exaggerate claims of disability involve physicians on both sides.

Sickness is . . . the leading excuse for employee absence in the U.S. . . . Unfortunately, there's no way to measure how many "sickness" absences are justified. . . . Cases of legitimately sick employees who prolong at-home recuperation at the company's expense pose another problem . . . most apt to occur when the ailing worker is left strictly to the care of his personal physician.[10]

An English insurance company physician observed, in a 1913 treatise on malingering, that the common law "gave the first impetus to . . . the practice of making much out of little; the various Workmen's Compensation Acts have still further enlarged this field."[11] One reason for this is to counteract the opposite tendency on the part of the sick or injured worker's adversaries at law. "The stricken soldier in industrial warfare . . . assumes that the State, or the insurance company by which his master is protected, will minimize his illness, and therefore he must exaggerate. . . . He looks to his own family doctor to support him against what he assumes to be a large and wealthy corporation."[12]

The question of malingering is raised not only by persons with an interest in enforcing labor discipline or in minimizing compensation in disability claims. A writer connected with a labor union that, in the 1970s in the United States probably has been most alert to workers' health and safety, commented:

Without doubt workers . . . sometimes do malinger, pretend to be hurt when they are not, exaggerate small pains into great ones. But there are countless cases . . . in which examination by private physicians have found ailments company doctors declared did not exist. The inevitable suspicion . . . is that company doctors permit the source of their fees to obscure their medical independence.[13]

On the one hand, a physician who serves as an agent of the employer or insurer is often despised and feared by the patients who feel ill served by him; on the other hand, the physician "who freely certifies for sick benefits is considered a kind man, and his appreciation by the working class is undoubted."[14]

While there is a built-in motive for malingering in hierarchic work organizations, the actual incidence of false or exaggerated claims is difficult to ascertain. In a British shop floor study published in 1971 of 2,367 work accidents, only three cases were seen in which a possibility of malingering existed. "Malingering may be seen as a problem by those who deal with serious injuries, but these are a tiny part of the accident spectrum. In our workshops . . . malingering was of no significance at all."[15] Nevertheless, there is no reason to doubt that a battle of wits between patients and company doctors is part of the ongoing class conflict. "Most workers are convinced," wrote Davidson, the union official quoted above, "that physicians serving the employers consistently interpret their findings so as to protect the company, rather than in such a way as to best serve the patient."[16] Given that perception of third-party medical practice in industry, exaggeration may in fact be a rational response in the adversary process.

COLLECTIVE BARGAINING AND GRIEVANCE PROCEDURES

The institutionalized structure of collective bargaining in the United States that was shaped under the aegis of the Wagner Act is of undoubted importance for the conflict over work hazards. Protection of concerted action by employees, legitimization of grievance procedures, and the legal existence of unions are essential to the struggle for a safe and healthful work environment.

One of the main channels for adjudication of disputes under formalized collective bargaining, the grievance machinery established by contractual agreement can be utilized when matters of safety and health are at issue. In a survey of health and safety provisions in 1,724 such agreements (in units covering 1,000 or more workers), material relevant to safety and health was found in over 93 percent of the documents examined. Implicit in all of them is the supposition that "the employee will not be required to work under unsafe or unhealthful conditions." Many of the contracts are explicit in this matter. In 371 agreements covering 1.9 million workers, the right to refuse to work under unsafe conditions or to demand being relieved from the job under such circumstances is recognized. In 42 agreements, the union is authorized to remove employees from the job, and in 301, the right to file health and safety grievances is codified (although presumably *any* contractual grievance machinery can be utilized for dealing with hazards or infractions). The standard interpretation of unsafe or unhealthful conditions involves "risks beyond those normally accepted as inherent in the job," though lack of consensus on acceptable risks is a perennial source of conflict.[17]

While little systematic research is available on the various issues subjected to grievance negotiation, inquiries to a number of corporations and unions provided some indication of the extent to which health and safety are disputed. The Oil, Chemical and Atomic Workers Union, one of the most active with respect to hazards in the workplace, reports that fewer than five percent of grievances filed by its constituent local unions deal with safety and health. The Bethlehem Steel Corporation found that of 14,250 grievances filed by steelworkers local unions in 1976, 380 (2.7 percent) involved safety and health, while in 1975, the proportion was 303 out of 13,155 (2.3 percent). During the same period at Bethlehem Steel, 21 of 196 grievances that went to arbitration (10.7 percent), were safety and health cases. During the four-year period 1973–76, 136 of 9,315 grievances in the Republic Steel Corporation (1.5 percent) were related to hazards, although there were reportedly more cases among these that sought to set aside disciplinary penalties for employee violations of safety rules than actual protests against unsafe conditions. In General Motors Corporation grievance records, 0.7 percent of cases in 1974 and 1.5 percent in 1975 were safety- or health-related. At Firestone Tire and Rubber, 1.8 percent of all grievances during a one-year period focused on hazard issues, while at B. F. Goodrich from 1971 to 1974, only 10 of 1,349 grievances (0.7 percent) fell under this category. At B. F. Goodrich there were no arbitrated safety cases since 1974, a fact attributed to establishment of a joint union and management committee that meets weekly to deal promptly with hazards brought to its attention.[18]

Beyond these cursory reports it is necessary to rely on arbitration cases for insights into the kinds of conflict channeled into the grievance procedures. One of the most persistent issues that recurs among health and safety arbitration cases is punishment invoked by management against employees whose refusal to work is based on a disputed claim of abnormal hazards. As noted above, the right to refuse work or to be relieved from the job under unsafe conditions is explicit in 21.5 percent of major collective bargaining agreements. The matter at arbitration is the grievance protesting the penalty, and the arguments revolve around the adversaries' perceptions of work hazards and the marshalling of evidence in support of those opposing perceptions.

A guiding principle of some arbitrators in resolving these cases is that if a worker who asks to be relieved or leaves his job acted in good faith and not for ulterior purposes, he may not be penalized. In other cases the perception and intentions of the worker have been deemed irrelevant. A worker does not "achieve immunity from discipline" for refusal to work because of the sincerity of his belief that he faced an extraordinary hazard. "Unless such imminent (immediate) danger to life or limb is satisfactorily demonstrated at the arbitration hearing, the refusal to undertake the work is insubordination."[19] Under either interpretation, the situation has to go beyond the "normal hazard inherent in the operation" in order to qualify as a hazard in this context.

Another topic that appears frequently among reported arbitration decisions is protective equipment, such as goggles, safety shoes, or special clothing. Conflict over safety equipment usually centers on the allocation of costs, and that conflict is nowhere more explicitly illuminated than in a 1951 grievance of United Auto Workers and Budd Company.[20] The complaint of the union was that failure to supply oil-resistant jackets and oil-repellent aprons to certain shipping employees was a violation of the collective bargaining agreement. One worker had been burned to death when his oil-soaked clothing was ignited while he warmed himself in front of a stove. The company claimed that it had spent $122,122 for safety items during the preceding year and that it would be "expensive to provide protective clothing for everyone." The union countered this by saying that the claimed expenditure came only to three cents per day per employee and the "health and safety of employees are worth more than the money." The arbitrator figured the expense at five cents per day rather than three, but ruled in favor of the union.

In one case a requirement that long-haired steelworkers who didn't tuck their hair into their hard hats must wear fire-resistant snoods led to a grievance against obliging the workers to pay for these snoods. The grievance was denied by the arbitrator.[21] Presumably the expense could be avoided by getting a haircut. In another case a reduction of the number of registered nurses in a steel mill was ruled by the arbitrator not to have been a violation of safety provisions in the contract.[22] In a case over refusal to work unless the employer provided protective clothing, an arbitrator observed that "resort to the grievance procedure is not an antidote to pneumonia,"[23] that is, workers should not have to await arbitration award to get adequate protection.

The 1974 coal miners' contract provides for establishment of mine health and safety committees composed of miners employed at the site who are empowered to remove all employees from an area in case of imminent danger. The employer "is required to follow the Committee's recommendation and remove the Employees from the area immediately." However, in the event the committee "acts arbitrarily and capriciously, a member or members may be removed from the committee."[24] Resolution of conflict over removal of members is then specified as subject to arbitration.

A union official points out the element of conflict inherent in the problem of workers' right to refuse to work under conditions of imminent danger: "On the one hand, unions cite numerous instances in which workers have been maimed or killed by operations which they had complained were dangerous; on the other, management is fearful that giving workers the right to 'red tag' would unduly interfere with production and would give workers another tool to solve unrelated grievances."[25]

At United States Steel a grievance was filed when the company decided to discontinue furnishing the union with copies of accident reports. The grievance was upheld by an arbitrator who commented that fear expressed by management that "the union might 'misuse' information" in the accident reports was without foundation.[26]

Only a small proportion of health and safety grievances, in arbitration or on the shop floor, deal with actual hazardous conditions, because the time lag may make this an impractical if not downright dangerous approach. In one case an unsafe method for operating metal-cutting shears was initiated by an employer, whereby the man controlling the shears could not see the other man employed in the process. This practice began on June 27, 1963, and the arbitrator ruled on February 7, 1964 that it was a violation of the safety provision in the contract. Seven months is an unconscionably long time to correct a dangerous condition.[27] Nevertheless, utilization of grievance procedures is a noteworthy if minor tactic in the conflict over industrial hazards that was not in evidence in the pre–World War I material discussed above. The same can be said for strikes.

If strikes are among the most visible expressions of industrial conflict it remains to be determined to what extent health and safety issues figure in precipitating work stoppages. The available data are from the tabulation of work stoppages published by the U.S. Bureau of Labor Statistics. These undoubtedly understate the importance of work hazards as sources of conflict, because many walkouts over excessive heat or unusual dangers are undoubtedly of short duration, perhaps involving only a small portion of the work force. These may never be reported to or by the government. Furthermore, in over one-half of all reported work stoppages, pay rates are at issue, and strikes have been more common in settling such contractual matters as pay adjustments than in other disputed areas. Nevertheless, it can be seen that a small but increasing proportion of reported work stoppages are attributed to safety measures, dangerous equipment, and related problems.

The official data on work stoppages obviously do not include such incidents as the refusal of four New York City air pollution control engineers to inspect factories in which products containing asbestos were manufactured.[28] Their refusal on the grounds that the city would not provide them with disposable protective clothing led to their being charged with incompetence and misconduct. This industrial action by professional staff members in a regulatory agency is as much a part of the struggle over work hazards as the strikes that appear in the official tabulations.

Sometimes the conflict is waged even within the federal government, as in the case of an administrative judge in the Department of the Interior who was officially reprimanded by an Assistant Secretary of the Interior for enforcing a coal mine safety penalty against a Kentucky coal company. The administrative judges' "trade union" supplied $5,000 for the legal appeals needed to remove the reprimand from the file of the reprimanded judge. "One irony in the dispute is that, while

TABLE 15. *U.S. Safety-Related Work Stoppages, 1966–1975*

Year	Total	Safety-Related	Percentage
1966	4,405	34	0.8
1967	4,595	45	1.0
1968	5,045	52	1.0
1969	5,700	78	1.4
1970	5,716	92	1.6
1971	5,138	75	1.5
1972	5,010	120	2.4
1973	5,353	155	2.9
1974	6,074	153	2.5
1975	5,031	165	3.3

SOURCES: For 1966, U.S. Bureau of Labor, Bureau of Labor Statistics, *Handbook of Labor Statistics, 1971*, p. 314; for 1967–74, *Handbook of Labor Statistics, 1976*, pp. 301–8; for 1975, *Work Stoppages 1975*, Summary 76–7, p. 7.

lawyers have wrangled here for nearly a year over the propriety of the reprimand to Judge Kennedy, the coal company . . . now faces court action . . . to collect not only the $2,682 assessment, but also about $30,000 in previously assessed fines for other mine safety infractions."[29]

The ramifications of the adversary process over hazards in the work environment are far-reaching indeed, when a Department of the Interior official had to utilize appeals procedures in the Justice Department for having enforced mine safety regulations. The ruling by Attorney General Edward Levi held that the reprimand had itself been an impropriety and that the enforcement decision that had occasioned it was a proper exercise of duty.

Exposure to lead in battery plants is a focal point of conflict as exemplified in a California factory where the state division of industrial safety imposed a $45,000 fine because airborne lead particles were found in quantities thirteen times the acceptable level. The management threatened to close up shop and move to a different state. The dilemma between productivity and safety was epitomized by the president of the union in the plant who commented, "Nobody wants to be out of a job but nobody wants to work in that environment. It's not right that we have to choose between our job and our health."[30]

OCCUPATIONAL SAFETY AND HEALTH ACT

The Occupational Safety and Health Act and the agency that is charged with its administration have been focal points of a raging conflict since the passage of the act. The provisions of the law provide new channels for adversary processes dealing with work hazards, and the agency has been under attack from interests that hold that it does too much and, until recently, from groups that think it does too little to implement the goals of the act. The manifestations of conflict in and around OSHA illuminate the theme of this study, as dramatized by the "Guadalupe" case.

About 5 P.M. on May 10, 1976, Jose Salazar Ramirez, a carding machine operator who worked under the name of Jose Guadalupe at the Thomas Hodgson and Sons yarn mill in Suncook, New Hampshire, was killed by the machine he was tending.[31] Upon hearing a cry a supervisor shut off the machine's power supply, but the worker's body had already been drawn into the rollers. The town police chief, upon his arrival at 5:16 P.M., summoned a Spanish-speaking priest from a nearby boys' home, who administered last rites to Guadalupe. The machine had to be dismantled to remove the body. The medical examiner ruled that death was caused by a crushed chest and internal hemorrhage.

Guadalupe, who was twenty-two, had come from Mexico in search of employment about three months prior to his death in the rollers of No. 8 card machine in the Hodgson mill. He had left his wife and child in the town of Vicente Guerrero, Durango, and lived with two of his brothers in Manchester. Hired on February 2, 1976, he worked on the 3 to 11 P.M. shift for $2.90 per hour and an attendance bonus of $20 per week. He was one of 275 employees in a factory where there was no union representation. While there had been no fatalities, during the year prior to his death there had been 87 nonfatal injuries in the mill, of which eighteen were lost-time injuries resulting in a loss of 223 work days (12.4 days average).

The compliance officer of the Occupational Safety and Health Administration began an investigation on the day following the accident and recommended a citation against the employer for serious violation of the general duty clause of the Occupational Safety and Health Act, which states: "The employer will furnish each of his employees employment and a place of employment which are free from recognized hazards that are causing or are likely to cause death or serious physical harm to his employees." The fatal injury resulted, according to the investigative report, while the employee was engaged in cleaning the brush roller of the card machine while the power was on and with the machine "in an operating mode." It was concluded that Guadalupe's hand was caught in the rollers which rotated in opposite directions at 250 r.p.m. and that his arm and part of his body were drawn in and crushed before the machine stopped. Absence of a written safety policy and reliance on verbal instructions were noted. Assessment of a $600 fine (the maximum of $1,000 for a serious violation minus a 40 percent adjustment factor) and immediate abatement of the hazard were ordered.

As provided by the law, the company through its legal counsel notified OSHA that it "contests the citation for serious violation and proposed penalty with respect thereto." The complaint was then placed on the docket for trial before an administrative law judge of the Occupational Safety and Health Review Commission. This led to adversary proceedings that illustrate both industrial hazards and their place in class conflict.

In a motion for discovery, the employer sought to ascertain the names of employees who had given written statements to the compliance officer during his investigation. The reason for this request was that,

as a result of the employee fatality and subsequent issuance of the citation, Respondent's relation with certain of its employees has been aggravated, and . . . if Respondent is forced to interview all employees who worked in the aforesaid area to determine which ones provided written statements to Compliance Officer Rogers, such action could be viewed by such employees to be a form of harassment, thereby adversely affecting the employment relations with such employees.

The inference seems quite clear that there was a desire on the part of the respondent to "interview" (and subject to what could be perceived as harassment) only those workers who were actually "guilty" of giving statements to the compliance officer. In opposition to this motion the state labor department attorneys argued that "the information sought by the respondent is privileged and need not be disclosed."

On July 27, 1976, the employer was served with a "request for admissions" from OSHA concerning the truth of thirty-nine statements of fact in the case. In reply, the employer admitted engaging in interstate commerce and having carding machines in its mill, the cleaning of which while in an operating mode was not recommended by the manufacturer of the machines. There were denials concerning the practice by carding machine operators of cleaning rollers while machines were "in an operating mode," of management's knowledge and acquiescence in this practice, and that workers who engaged in this practice did so under instructions from management. As for Guadalupe, it was admitted that he neither spoke nor could read English, and that there had been no written safety program in either English or Spanish for the operation of carding machines. It was also admitted that none of his immediate supervisors spoke Spanish and that he had had no experience with carding machines before he was hired at the Hodgson mill. The fact that the fatal carding machine "comes to a complete stop one and one-half to two minutes after being deenergized" was admitted. On the other hand, the employer "neither admits nor denies" that Guadalupe was cleaning the machine while it was in an operating mode.

The adversaries then exchanged lists of the witnesses whom they planned to call at the forthcoming trial. One employer witness was to testify about the training instruction given to Guadalupe. The witness maintained that while working under his supervision, Guadalupe did not attempt to clean the card machine while in operation and that another employee had been dismissed for failure to obey the prohibition against cleaning a machine while in operation.

The OSHA case centered on the charge of "permitting the practice of employees cleaning card machine No. 8 while it was in an operating mode." The employer's attorney countered by arguing that "a condition which has caused an isolated fatality does not by virtue of such fatality rise to the level of a 'recognized hazard.' A single incident of so cleaning No. 8 card machine, assuming such an incident could be proved, which Respondent does not concede, would not constitute proof that any practice existed." The administrative law judge overruled employer objections to a number of the requests for admission.

On September 24 attorneys for both sides met in a pretrial conference with the judge, during which they summarized their respective arguments. The OSHA counsel argued that Guadalupe had not been provided with safe employment, since he was permitted to attempt to clean the machine "without adequate training, supervision and sanctioning. Guadalupe, a Spanish-speaking man, could not understand spoken or written English, matters known to respondent; yet the one member of respondent's supervisory staff who could speak Spanish . . . was on duty only a portion of Guadalupe's regular shift." The employer's case rested on the claim that cleaning the machine while the rollers were rotating had been forbidden for "about a year prior to May 10, 1976." In about ten years of operation there had been no injury resulting from cleaning a running carding machine and nobody knows how the fatality occurred; "and from mere occurrence, employer liability may not be inferred."

The case never came to trial. On November 22 the employer withdrew the contest against the citation and entered a consent decree. It contained an agreement to "tender to the Secretary of Labor the amount of $600 in full payment of the proposed penalty." It was stipulated that nothing contained in the settlement "shall constitute evidence or an admission . . . of any wrongdoing or misconduct or liability on the part of Respondent . . . except in proceeding brought by the Secretary of Labor." The stipulation was included in case the widow might file suit against the company. Should she do so, it would be absolutely critical to the defense that the stipulation not contain any admission that an OSHA standard or statute has been violated."

The importance of this case lies in the fact that it illustrates the workings of a newly established framework for the ongoing conflict over work hazards. The enactment in 1970 of the Occupational Safety and Health Act created a new regulatory agency whose enforcement activities augment the previously existing vehicles for adversary processes concerning health and safety. Though in a case like the death of Jose Guadalupe, inspection would be initiated almost immediately by the agency, one of the most important sources of information for OSHA stems from the provision of the law that provides for (and protects) reporting by employees on health and safety violations in their place of employment.

Worker participation in policing the working environment is anathema to many conservative interests. Dan Smoot, a spokesman of the extreme right, charged that unions seek stringent implementation of OSHA standards because this would "provide an almost limitless number of contentious issues . . . to bludgeon management into concessions on matters that having nothing to do with the health and safety of employees."[32] In Britain even more colorful language was used by a member of Parliament in a House of Commons debate on accident inspection by workers' committees, which would create "a sea-lawyer's paradise, giving a wonderful opportunity to those who want to make trouble and disrupt our industries, where all strikes have failed. Under the guise of safety it will be possible to delay matters while an inspection is made."[33]

It is a common allegation of opponents to employee participation in health and safety standards enforcement that complaint procedures will be used for ulterior purposes or in

TABLE 16. *Validity of Health and Safety Complaints to OSHA, 1973–1976*

Fiscal Year	Safety Complaints			Health Complaints		
	Received	Valid	Percentage Valid	Received	Valid	Percentage Valid
1973	7,070	6,452	91.2	—	—	
1974	4,552	4,315	94.8	2,171	2,091	96.3
1975	5,016	4,725	94.7	2,242	2,148	95.8
1976	6,631	6,427	96.9	3,262	3,153	96.6

SOURCE: Dr. Eula Bingham, U.S. Assistant Secretary of Labor, to author, June 8, 1977.

order to achieve goals that may be elusive by other means. This contention is not supported by the evidence of complaints to the Occupational Safety and Health Administration. The agency judged that 94.7 percent of health and safety complaints were valid, and there is no evidence that the remainder were filed for ulterior purposes.

The high proportion of employee complaints found to be valid should come as no surprise. While the names of complaining employees are concealed from their employers on request, they are known to the regulatory agency. Hardly anyone would trifle with the power of the federal government by making frivolous complaints and no prudent person would knowingly send an OSHA compliance officer on a wild goose chase.

An OSHA official pointed out that since "there would always be too many work places and too few Compliance Officers" for effective implementation of the law, the worker on the job had to be viewed as "a first line Compliance Officer" to call attention to hazards in the workplace. However, a byproduct of this right and duty is the possibility of employer reprisals against subordinates who make complaints. In order to protect employees, Section 11(c) of OSHA prohibits discrimination for participation in proceedings under the act and provides procedures for adjudicating complaints of discrimination. This is an added dimension of the institutional framework for conflict over work hazards.

Reprisals against complaining employees have included discharge, demotion, assignment to undesirable shifts, denial of promotion, loss of benefits, assignment of more onerous duties, surveillance, harassment, blacklisting, and other deprivations. During a three-year period, 20.6 percent of discrimination complaints under Section 11(c) were judged by the enforcement agency to have merit (excluding cases withdrawn by the complaining employee). Some of these were settled through negotiations conducted by the agency, and the remainder were referred for litigation by the regional Solicitors of Labor.

TABLE 17. *Complaints of Discrimination under Section 11(c)(1) of OSHA*

Disposition	Fiscal 1975	Fiscal 1976	Fiscal 1977[*]
Dismissed	493 (84.0%)	853 (75.6%)	895 (80.8%)
Settled	28 (4.8%)	99 (8.8%)	93 (8.4%)
Referred for litigation	66 (11.2%)	176 (15.6%)	120 (10.8%)
Total processed[†]	587	1127	1108
Withdrawn	117	594	702
Total received	704	1721	1810

SOURCE: A. A. Denhard, Jr., Baltimore, Md., (OSHA Review Officer), to author, June 29, 1977.
[*] To June 17, 1977
[†] Excludes cases withdrawn by complainants

In an illustrative case documentation of which was supplied (with names deleted) under the Freedom of Information Act, the procedures for settlement of discrimination complaints can be seen.[34] A woman who had been employed as a book-keeper by a Pittsburgh tobacco and candy wholesaler was discharged for complaining to OSHA about cold temperatures in the warehouse where she worked and about the lack of a separate toilet for women. Even though the agency refused to divulge to the employer the name of the complainant, since there were only seven employees (including two women) in the enterprise, after a campaign of harassment the woman was discharged. She sought redress under the provisions of 11(c)(2) of the OSHA, which states that if after "investigation the Secretary [of Labor] determines that the provisions of this subsection have been violated, he shall bring an action in any appropriate United States district court."

The investigators, after interviewing the complainant, her former employer and several witnesses, determined that a strong case existed and persuaded the employer to enter into an out-of-court settlement, thus avoiding costly litigation. Under its terms, the discharged bookkeeper was offered reinstatement in the enterprise, which she declined, and $1,420 in back pay, which she accepted. In addition, the employer was obligated to post a notice of settlement for the information of the other employees. This notice, as required by law, contained a promise that the employer would not "in any manner interfere with, restrain or coerce" any employee for exercising rights stipulated by OSHA. The notice also stated that full reinstatement of the complaining employee had been offered and declined, and that she had been "made whole for all monies and benefits lost as a result of her termination and have purged her personnel record of all derogatory references related thereto."

In another discrimination case adjudicated by OSHA, the sort of conflict entailed by the complaint procedures under the act becomes quite obvious. In the Notice to Employees that the OSHA Review Officer ordered the employer to post, after the routine statement that the employer henceforth "will not interfere with, restrain, or coerce any employee" for exercising his rights under the act, the following appeared:

WE WILL NOT THREATEN WITH BODILY INJURY OR IN ANY OTHER MANNER ⌊NAME DELETED⌋ IN REPRISAL FOR HIS EXERCISE OF THE RIGHTS DESCRIBED ABOVE.

WE WILL NOT INTERROGATE EMPLOYEES TO ATTEMPT TO DETERMINE WHO MADE COMPLAINTS CONCERNING SAFETY AND HEALTH MATTERS TO THE OCCUPATIONAL SAFETY AND HEALTH ADMINISTRATION.

WE WILL EXPUNGE FROM ANY PERSONNEL RECORDS MAINTAINED ON ⌊NAME DELETED⌋ ANY DEROGATORY REFERENCE TO THE EXERCISE OF HIS PROTECTED RIGHTS DESCRIBED ABOVE.[35]

Since the required public notice promised the employer would refrain from threatening bodily harm, it is obvious that the complainant had presented evidence of such threats at his hearings.

The adversary processes in the Guadalupe case under the general duty clause of the act and in the cases under 11(c)(2) show how institutional channels for conflict were provided by the law. However, the law itself has been a focal point of conflict, both prior to and since its passage. The final version of the law passed by Congress reflects, as does presumably all legislation, the result of lobbying by opposing interests. Since the law went into effect, these same interests have continued to battle over attempts to weaken or strengthen the act. The ongoing contention over OSHA is very much a part of the overall conflict over work hazards.

A Teamsters Union publication taxed OSHA officials for an "attitude that shows priority compassion for problems and inconveniences of management."[36] Automobile Workers' leader Leonard Woodcock further articulated dissatisfaction: "OSHA constituted an official commitment that the millions of American working men and women who are on the cutting, poisoning and killing edge of our industrial society would for the first time enjoy the simple but human right to a workplace free of hazards. But the government has reneged on its promise to protect its working citizens."[37] The reasons given for this negative assessment included inadequate funding, efforts to turn over enforcement to state agencies, excessive delays in inspections, inadequate standards, and a greater concern for economic feasibility than for human lives.

One OSHA official responded to this crossfire from critics right and left by saying: "Since the criticism of the OSHA program is about equal from all sides, we are probably steering a right course toward accomplishing the objectives of the act."[38] This reaction implies that the mission is to find a middle ground in an arena of class conflict, rather than to achieve a working environment free from recognized hazards. Another critique that OSHA is doing too little was published by the Health Research Group in 1975, based on agency performance reports. OSHA is taken to task because so few violations are classified as serious (1.2 percent in 1974) and because the penalties for serious violations are too low (an average of $582 in 1974). For the 98.5 percent of violations deemed nonserious the penalties averaged $13.33. The small proportion of establishments under the agency's jurisdiction inspected at least once—3.8 percent in the aggregate activity of four years—is criticized as well. Among 1,826 contested cases in fiscal 1975, 12 percent of citations were withdrawn and 34 percent modified; for a total of $702,710 in proposed penalties, the regional Solicitors of Labor granted a 69 percent reduction to $215,816. The time lag in the Occupational Safety and Health Review Commission averaged 217 days per case in 1974 and 231 in 1975, delays which were also criticized and OSHA was charged with "irresponsible inaction and callous insensitivity to the workers' need for effective protection from workplace hazards."[39] The low level of inspection activity and the minimal penalties, according to this view are counterproductive to the mandate of the agency:

Maximum compliance is achieved when there is a high probability of detection (inspection) and severe penalties. Unfortunately, OSHA has not compensated for its low inspection probability by issuing appropriately severe penalties. Moreover, it has not sufficiently increased enforcement staff to increase the probability of inspection. The result is an enforcement effort which sanctions violations with impunity.[40]

In marked contrast to union charges against OSHA, for example, claiming that the agency does not do enough to assure safety and health, the extreme right has made the Occupational Safety and Health Administration a prime target for vilification. For example, the right claims that OSHA, created by Congress with "unlimited, unconstitutional police-state powers" has the potential "to become the worst atrocity against American constitutional government ever committed," by imposing penalties in violation of the due process clause of the Fifth Amendment and without right of trial by jury in violation of the Sixth Amendment.[41] Dan Smoot wrote that "many OSHA actions against employers reflect a vengeful attitude toward businessmen, while others seem to reflect merely the exasperating silliness of bureaucracy." The agency "could harass all American private business out of existence."[42] In a statement before the House Select Committee on Labor, a spokesman for the Liberty Lobby argued:

There is no freedom in free enterprise so long as the federal government can come in unannounced and dictate to the employer concerning his operation. . . . In Russia, Lenin forced out the entrepreneur "for the benefit of the workers"; in Italy, Mussolini tried it allegedly for "grandeur." Now here in the U.S., Labor Department bureaucrats are squeezing the small businessman out and destroying private enterprise in the name of "safety." The issue is not safety and health—it is socialism vs. free enterprise. We support repeal of the Occupational Safety and Health Act.[43]

Repeal of the Occupational Safety and Health Act is also a high-priority goal of the American Conservative Union. In a strident warning against the "OSHSTAPO" one writer suggested that "the real purpose of OSHA is . . . to shut down small business, in order to give total control of our economy to the millionaire Socialists who mean to rule us."[44] With a more cautious approach the Chamber of Commerce of the United States in 1977 advocated elimination of fines against first offenders in nonserious violations, a "grandfather clause" to exempt existing equipment from regulations, and enforcement of orders during the appeals process. While its rhetoric is less flamboyant, the intent is similar.

The decisions of federal courts are, as we have seen, of great importance in the conflicts occasioned by the regulations and decisions of OSHA. Two decisions concerning toxic substances in the work environment underscore the vital role of the judiciary.

In a case arising out of industry appeals against a standard for coke oven emissions, *American Iron and Steel Institute, et al. v. OSHA*, the United States Court of Appeals for the Third Circuit in 1978 rejected the industry contention that the Secretary of Labor had ignored the economic feasibility question and observed that implementation of the standard would raise the cost of steel one half of one percent:

Although we are very sensitive to the financial implications of the standard . . . we are not persuaded that its implementation would precipitate anything approaching the "massive dislocation" . . .

which would characterize an economically infeasible standard. The secretary had sufficient data from which he could properly balance the cost to industry against the health needs of its employees. . . . We find no basis to conclude that the Secretary has not fulfilled his duty to inquire into the economic feasibility of the standard, nor are we persuaded that the standard is, in fact, infeasible. We also attach significance to the United Steelworkers' strong support of the standard.[45]

The steel industry employers in this case sought relief from a 0.5 percent cost increment while the collective bargaining agency of the steelworkers sought relief from a health hazard of incalculable cost to its potential victims.

Finally, in a 5 to 4 decision in the "benzene" case, *Industrial Union Department* v. *American Petroleum Institute et al.*, the United States Supreme Court in 1980 invalidated an OSHA standard that reduced the allowable worker exposure to benzene in the air—a cause of leukemia and other diseases—from ten parts per million to one part per million. Implementation of the lower standard would have entailed a cost of $500,000,000. The court upheld the industry appeal against the new rule on the grounds of insufficient medical evidence. Where there is a doubt, according to the prevailing view, the benefit of the doubt goes toward minimizing entrepreneurial costs despite the demonstrable risk of social costs in the form of benzene-induced cases of leukemia and other diseases.

The dissenting opinion by Mr. Justice Marshall, in which Justices Brennan, White, and Blackmun concurred, assailed the plurality view as a flagrant disregard of the restriction on judicial authority and contrary to the "plain meaning" of OSHA, "based only on the plurality's solicitude for the welfare of regulated industries."[46] Thus, the crucial role of regulatory agencies in the conflict over allocation of costs is brought into sharp focus.

While science has determined that exposure to benzene at levels above 1ppm creates a definite risk of health impairment, the magnitude of the risk cannot be quantified at the present time. The risk at

issue has hardly been shown to be insignificant; indeed, future research may reveal that the risk is in fact considerable. But the existing evidence may frequently be inadequate to enable the Secretary to
make the threshold finding of "significance" that the Court requires
today. If so, the consequence of the plurality's approach would be to
subject American workers to a continuing risk of cancer and other
fatal diseases, and to render the Federal Government powerless to
take protective action on their behalf. Such an approach *would place
the burden of medical uncertainty squarely on the shoulders of the
American worker.*[47]

Mr. Justice Marshall evoked a reminder from a 1905 dissent by
Mr. Justice Holmes that the Constitution "does not enact Mr.
Herbert Spencer's Social Statics" (that holy writ of laissez
faire); Marshall concluded that "responsibility to scrutinize
federal administrative action does not authorize this Court to
strike its own balance between the costs and benefits of occupational safety standards."[48] Here again we see epitomized
the whole conflict over work hazards: the avoidance of entrepreneurial costs by one side entails imposition of social
costs on the other—an imposition that will be resisted.

CONCLUSION

Douglas Fraser, head of the United Automobile Workers, has
referred to the controversy raging over OSHA as a "one-sided
class war."[49] It is certainly an unequal struggle, part of the
ongoing conflict that embraces the whole complex of issues
and problems arising out of work hazards. Several conclusions
from the material of this study bear on Fraser's characterization of this conflict. First, the conflict is less one-sided now
than in the first decades of the century. Second, the legal
framework is crucial in shaping the relevant adversary processes and the laws themselves are a focus of conflict. Third,
the conflict over work hazards is a condition endemic in the
industrial mode of production.

The conflict is less one-sided today because of the accession
of the manual labor force to political citizenship with an attendant capability of influencing legislation. Workmen's compen-

sation has greatly diminished the proportion of the victims of work hazards who are sent away empty-handed. The Wagner Act provisions that survived the gutting of that landmark labor law after World War II have provided a basis for collective bargaining and for union strength that have had tremendous direct and indirect consequences for dealing with work hazards. Strikes, grievance negotiations, and arbitration cases are by no means the most salient of these consequences. The unionized worker has a higher status than his pre–Wagner Act predecessors, and treatment as a disposable or "throw-away" factor is a fate more easily imposed the lower the worker's status. Moreover, the strengthening of unions has enabled them to bring to bear effective support on legislation such as OSHA. The Occupational Safety and Health Act of 1970 was shaped in part by the pressure exerted by unions. It provided a whole new range of options and channels for carrying on the conflict for a safer and more healthful work environment, and in turn it has served to move up safety and health in the bargaining agenda of many unions.

The importance of the legal framework of this conflict should not be underestimated. In view of what Gouldner has called "a continual temptation for the rich and powerful to minimize compliance with their obligations and to maximize their rights," existence of laws and of law enforcement is crucial.[50] Law defines obligations and law enforcement constrains compliance. Without this protection the casualties who run afoul of work hazards would be immeasurably more disadvantaged. Even the egregious Employers' Liability Laws were not perceived as an unmitigated evil by unions that preferred to see them amended rather than replaced by no-fault compensation laws. Arbitrary exercise of managerial prerogative unrestrained by industrial laws and by state power would make exploitation far more onerous. Moreover, the compulsion of law serves to protect more humane employers from going under in competition with less humane competitors.

There is an endemic conflict of interest between the workers at risk in manual labor occupations and the employers and managers who arrogate to themselves the decisions as to what constitutes acceptable risks. Acceptable to whom and on what grounds? This conflict is endemic because reducing the speed and intensity of labor effort or the length of the working day in order to reduce injuries, elimination of certain materials from the work environment in order to reduce occupational disease, and providing appliances, materials and procedures to assure the safety and health of workers all entail *costs*. The economic impact of these costs is inevitably a matter of contention. Since this problem is a consequence of the technology and social organization of industrial production, there is no reason to suppose that work hazards are less a source of conflict under state socialism than under capitalist property relations. The decision as to what constitutes an acceptable risk is invariably made by the bureaucrat in an office, and it matters little if the bureaucrat was co-opted from the shop floor.

The dilemma between safety and productivity that is inherent in the mode of production and the unequal apportionment of risk that is inherent both in the hierarchic control structures and the complex division of labor support the conclusion that the clash of interests arising from work hazards is endemic in industrial societies. How this conflict manifests itself in a democratic capitalist society has been elaborated above. Its manifestations under state socialism are shrouded by a veil of censorship, but it is reasonable to assume that where the official trade unions are agencies of management, the problem may be the more intractable for being denied.

At one level we may view the dilemma of safety and productivity in Maslow's terms. At some point safety needs may interfere with satisfaction of the physiological needs ranking highest in the hierarchy of needs. In other words, if being perfectly safe requires staying home and never venturing out of bed, we will starve to death. Thus it is indeniable that safety and health programs have an economic impact and the struggle over work hazards will be an endless quest for compromise rather than for a definitive solution.

Nelson Rockefeller asserted in connection with an incident involving radiation hazards that "you can't have riskless society."[51] That is undeniable. Thus there will always be a problem of minimizing the dangers of the workplace, assessing alternative techniques, and juggling with the dilemma of safety and productivity.

If there can be no such thing as a riskless society then the distribution of these risks is a matter of grave import. Are the risks faced by the Rockefellers of this world similar to the risks faced by the manual labor force? So long as hazards of work fall disproportionately on one class, so long as higher-ups can make glib pronouncements about the inevitability of risks from which they themselves are sheltered, but which take a fearful toll among industrial workers, so long will industrial hazards be a focal point of conflict.

Inequalities in life chances are at issue, and those who are relegated to the more hazardous jobs have interests both in abatement of the risks and abatement of the disparities between the hazards they face and those faced by the privileged and powerful. When these interests are consciously pursued, conflict develops. From the historical and contemporary case materials presented in this book, it can be seen that while part of this conflict takes the form of grievances, strikes, and other activities within the enterprise, in the United States this is predominantly a conflict that has been channeled into the political institution. The courts, workmen's compensation boards, the Occupational Safety and Health Administration, and other agencies are vehicles by which the ongoing conflict over safety and health in the workplace is pursued.

Notes

PREFACE

1. E. H. Phelps Brown, *The Growth of British Industrial Relations* (London: Macmillan, 1965), p. 74.

2. Ralph Nader, "Introduction," in Joseph A. Page and Mary-Win O'Brien, *Bitter Wages* (New York: Grossman, 1973), p. xiii.

3. Dwight Manufacturing Company Papers, vol. HL3, March 31, 1908, Baker Library, Harvard University, Cambridge, Mass.

CHAPTER I

1. "Jailing of Plant Director in Workers' Death Raises Storm in France," *New York Times*, October 5, 1975; "M. Jean Chapron est remis en liberté," *Le Monde*, 5–6 October, 1975; "Pourquoi M. Charette a fait un éclat," *Le Point*, October 6, 1975; "M. Jean Chapron a été relaxé . . ." *Le Monde*, July 2, 1976.

2. "Italian industrialists jailed over use of chemicals that killed eight workers," *Times* (London), June 22, 1977.

3. *New York Times*, February 16, 1978, p. 1; August 19, 1979, p. B3.

4. *New York Times*, May 7, 1978, sec. 1, p. 26.

5. *New York Times*, December 1, 1977, p. A12; December 21, 1977, p. A6; *Times* (London), July 24, 1980, p. 9.

6. Adriano Tilgher, *Homo Faber* (Chicago: Regnery, 1964), p. 3; Hannah Arendt, *The Human Condition* (Chicago: University of Chicago Press, 1958), p. 80n.

7. Max Weber, *Economy and Society*, ed. Guenther Roth and Claus Wittich (New York: Bedminster, 1968), p. 302.

8. Max Weber, *From Max Weber*, ed. Hans Gerth and C. Wright Mills (New York: Oxford University Press, 1958), p. 181.

9. R. H. Tawney, *Equality* (New York: Capricorn, 1961), pp. 60–62.

10. E. P. Thompson, *The Making of the English Working Class* (New York: Random House, 1963), p. 9.

11. Emile Durkheim, *Division of Labor in Society* (New York: Macmillan, 1933), p. 386; Emile Durkheim, *Professional Ethics and Civic Morals* (Glencoe: Free Press, 1958), p. 211.

12. E. A. Ross, *Principles of Sociology* (New York: Appleton-Century, 1930), p. 121.

13. Alvin Gouldner, "The Norm of Reciprocity: A Preliminary Statement," *American Sociological Review* 25 (April 1960): 167.

14. Eugene E. Ruyle, "Slavery, Surplus and Stratification on the Northwest Coast: The Ethnoenergetics of an Incipient Stratification System," *Current Anthropology* 14 (December 1973): 607.

15. Ibid.

16. John Foster, *Class Struggle in the Industrial Revolution* (London: Weidenfeld and Nicolson, 1974), p. 73.

17. Martin Bulmer, ed., *Working-Class Images of Society* (London: Routledge and Kegan Paul, 1975), p. 5.

18. E. J. Hobsbawm, "Class Consciousness in History," in Istvan Meszaros, ed., *Aspects of History and Class Consciousness* (New York: Herder, 1972), p. 11.

19. E. P. Thompson, *Making of the English Working Class*, p. 10.

20. Ellen Meiksins Woods, *Mind and Politics* (Berkeley: University of California Press, 1972), p. 111.

21. Jeremy Bentham, *Economic Writings*, vol. 3. (London: Allen and Unwin, 1952–54), p. 423.

22. C. B. Macpherson, *Political Theory of Possessive Individualism* (London: Oxford University Press, 1962), pp. 262–63.

23. A. D. Lindsay, "Individualism," *Encyclopedia of Social Science*, vol. 7 (New York: Macmillan, 1932), p. 674.

24. Alan Dawley, *Class and Community: The Industrial Revolution in Lynn* (Cambridge: Harvard University Press, 1976), p. 174.

25. Barrington Moore, Jr., *Injustice: The Social Bases of Obedience and Revolt* (White Plains, N.Y.: Sharpe, 1978), pp. 458–59, 471.

26. William L. Prosser, *Handbook of the Law of Torts*, 2nd ed. (St. Paul, Minn.: West, 1955), p. 6.

27. Abraham Maslow, *Motivation and Personality* (New York: Harper and Row, 1954), pp. 80–89.

28. Erik Olin Wright, *Class, Crisis and the State* (London: New Left Books, 1978), pp. 89–90.

29. Daniel Bell, *Cultural Contradictions of Capitalism* (New York: Basic Books, 1976), p. 189; Dewey Anderson and Percy Davidson, *Ballots and the Democratic Class Struggle* (Stanford: Stanford University Press, 1943); E. J. Hobsbawm, "Peasants and Politics," *Journal of Peasant Studies* 1 (October 1973): 13.

30. T. H. Marshall, *Class, Citizenship, and Social Development* (Garden City, N.Y.: Doubleday, 1965), p. 182.

31. Eugene Genovese, *Roll, Jordan, Roll* (New York: Random House, 1974), p. 621.

32. Henry S. Bennett, *Life on the English Manor* (Cambridge: Cambridge University Press, 1956), p. 100.

33. William H. Moreland, *The Agrarian System of Moslem India* (Delhi: Oriental Book Reprint Company, 1968), p. 207.

34. Morton H. Fried, *The Fabric of Chinese Society* (New York: Praeger, 1953), p. 105.

35. Clark Kerr, "Industrial Conflict and its Mediation," *American Journal of Sociology* 60 (November 1954): 231.

36. Marshall, *Class, Citizenship, and Social Development*, p. 188.

37. Durkheim, *Division of Labor*, p. 325.

38. Hilde Behrend, "The Effort Bargain," *Industrial and Labor Relations Review* 10 (July 1957): 505.

39. Arthur Kornhauser, Robert Dubin, and Arthur M. Ross, eds., *Industrial Conflict* (New York: McGraw-Hill, 1954), p. 13.

40. Kerr, "Industrial Conflict," p. 232.

41. R. H. Tawney, *The Acquisitive Society* (New York: Harcourt, 1920), p. 40.

42. W. Wesolowski, "The Notion of Strata and Class in Socialist Society," in A. Beteille, ed., *Social Inequality* (Baltimore: Penguin, 1969), p. 135.

43. Mary McAuley, *Labour Disputes in Soviet Russia 1957–1965* (Oxford: Clarendon Press, 1969), p. 101.

44. Walter Galenson, "Soviet Russia," in Kornhauser, et al., eds., *Industrial Conflict*, p. 478.

45. Harry Braverman, *Labor and Monopoly Capital* (New York: Monthly Review Press, 1974), p. 12.

46. Maurice Dobb, *Wages* (Cambridge: Cambridge University Press, 1966), p. 56.

47. Adam Smith, *Wealth of Nations* (New York: Modern Library, 1937), p. 80.

48. Dobb, *Wages*, p. 53.

49. Smith, *Wealth of Nations*, p. 80.

50. Genovese, *Roll, Jordan, Roll*, p. 520.

51. Karl Marx, *Capital*, vol. 1 (New York: Modern Library, n.d.) pp. 526, 535, 541.

52. James G. O'Hara, "Foreword," in Jerome B. Gordon, Alan Akman, and Michael L. Brooks, *Industrial Safety Statistics: A Re-Examination* (New York: Praeger, 1971), p. v.

53. Jeanne M. Stellman and Susan M. Daum, *Work Is Dangerous to Your Health* (New York: Random House, 1973), p. 8.

54. Joseph A. Page and Mary-Win O'Brien, *Bitter Wages* (New York: Grossman, 1973), p. 47.

55. Ray Davidson, *Peril on the Job* (Washington, D.C.: Public Affairs Press, 1970), pp. 172–73.

56. 3 OSHC 1820 at 1830, n.39.

57. K. William Kapp, *The Social Costs of Private Enterprise* (New York: Schocken, 1975), pp. 13–14.

58. Ibid., p. 47.

CHAPTER 2

1. Quoted in Edward Abbott Parry, *The Law and the Poor* (London: Smith, Elder, 1914), p. 86; Harry E. Mock, *Industrial Medicine and Surgery* (Philadelphia: Saunders, 1917), p. 130.

2. Interstate Commerce Commission, Bureau of Transportation Economics and Statistics, *Accident Bulletin #119* (Washington, D.C.: Government Printing Office, 1951); U.S. Bureau of Mines, *Injury Experience in Coal Mining, 1948,* Bulletin 509 (Washington, D.C.: Government Printing Office, 1952); U.S. Congress, 61st Congr., 2nd sess., Senate Document 633, *Immigrants in Industries,* pt. 1, vol. 1 (Washington, D.C.: Government Printing Office, 1910), p. 213.

3. J. T. Arlidge, *The Hygiene, Diseases and Mortality of Occupations* (London: Percival, 1892), pp. 360–61.

4. Ibid., p. 356.

5. U.S. Congress, 61st Congr., 2nd Sess., Senate Document 645, *Woman and Child Wage-Earners in the United States,* vol. 1 (Washington, D.C.: Government Printing Office, 1910), p. 374.

6. Massachusetts Senate Document No. 250, *Continuation of the Investigation of Conditions Affecting the Health and Safety of Employees in Factories and Other Establishments* (Boston: Wright and Potter, 1907), p. 8.

7. *Woman and Child Wage-Earners,* vol. 1, p. 366.

8. Ibid., pp. 370–71.

9. Ibid., pp. 369, 374.

10. Quoted by Eliot Freidson, "The Organization of Medical Practice," in Howard E. Freeman, et al., eds., *Handbook of Medical Sociology* (Englewood Cliffs, N.J.: Prentice-Hall, 1963), p. 300.

11. Mock, *Industrial Medicine,* p. 91.

12. Harry E. Mock, "Surgery in Industry," *Occupational Medicine* 2 (July 1946): pp. 50–51.

13. Alice Hamilton, *Exploring the Dangerous Trades* (Boston: Little, Brown, 1943), pp. 3–4.

14. David L. Edsall, "Medical-Industrial Relations and the War," *Johns Hopkins Hospital Bulletin* 29 (September 1918): 198.

15. *Woman and Child Wage-Earners,* vol. 1, pp. 391–92.

16. Massachusetts State Board of Health, *Thirty-Eighth Annual Report* (Boston: Wright and Potter, 1907), p. 478.

17. Ibid., p. 478.

18. Magnus Alexander, quoted in Winthrop L. Marvin, *Bulletin of the National Wool Manufacturers Association,* Boston, 1917, p. 80.

19. Crystal Eastman, *Work-Accidents and the Law* (New York: Charities Publication Committee, 1910), p. 84 (reprinted, New York: Arno, 1969).

20. Ibid., p. 94.

21. Ibid., p. 107.

22. Daniel L. Cease, "Compulsory Compensation for Injured Workmen," *American Labor Legislation Review* 1 (January 1911): 42.

23. David S. Beyer, *Accident Prevention in the Textile Industry* (New York: American Society of Mechanical Engineers, 1917), pp. 3–4.

24. Frederick L. Hoffman, "Industrial Accidents and Industrial Diseases," *Publications of the American Statistical Association* 11 (December 1909): 570.

25. Home Office Accidents Committee, "Report of the Departmental Committee on Accidents in Places under the Factory and Workshops Act," vol. 2, Minutes of Evidence and Appendix in *British Sessional Papers*, (1911) vol. 23 (London: Stationery Office, 1911), p. 325.

26. Ibid., vol. 1, p. 18.

27. Ibid., p. 13.

28. Ibid., p. 35.

29. Ibid., vol. 2, p. 213.

30. Massachusetts Commission to Investigate the Inspection of Factories, Workshops, Mercantile Establishments and Other Buildings, 1910, "Hearing Transcript, July 1–November 5, 1910," typescript (Boston: State House Library) pp. 257–59.

31. *Woman and Child Wage-Earners*, vol. 19, p. 98.

32. Ibid., p. 101.

33. Massachusetts Commission to Investigate the Inspection of Factories, Workshops, Mercantile Establishments and Other Buildings, *Report* (Boston: Wright and Potter, 1911), pp. 53, 59.

34. Quoted in Eastman, *Work-Accidents*, p. 106.

35. Massachusetts Revised Laws, 1902, ch. 106, 52.

36. Massachusetts Commission to Investigate the Inspection of Factories, Workshops, Mercantile Establishments and Other Buildings, 1910, "Hearing Transcript," pp. 369–70.

37. *Immigrants in Industries*, pt. 1, vol. 1, p. 233.

38. Hamilton, *Exploring the Dangerous Trades*, p. 152.

39. Ibid., p. 5.

40. *Immigrants in Industries*, pt. 3, p. 123.

41. Melvin Thomas Copeland, *The Cotton Manufacturing Industry in the United States* (Cambridge: Harvard University Press, 1912), p. 127.

42. *Immigrants in Industries*, pt. 3, p. 123.

43. See Sidney Pollard, *The Genesis of Modern Management* (Cambridge: Harvard University Press, 1962), p. 162; Herbert Gutman, "Work, Culture and Society in Industrializing America, 1815–1919," *American Historical Review* 78 (June 1973): 540.

44. Aumann to Golden, September 16, 1915, Dwight Manufacturing Company Collection, Baker Library, Harvard University. Cambridge, Mass.

45. *Woman and Child Wage-Earners*, vol. 1, p. 610.

46. Edward O'Donnell in *American Federationist* 4 (October 1897): 186–87, reprinted in W. Eliot Brownlee and Mary M. Brownlee, eds., *Women in the American Economy* (New Haven, Conn.: Yale University Press, 1976), p. 213ff.

47. *Woman and Child Wage-Earners*, vol. 1, p. 611.

48. Arthur Reed Perry, *Preventable Death in Cotton Manufacturing Industry*, U.S. Department of Labor, Bureau of Labor Statistics Bulletin No. 251 (Washington, D.C.: Government Printing Office, 1919), p. 81.

49. Massachusetts Commission to Investigate the Inspection of Factories, Workshops, Mercantile Establishments and Other Buildings, 1910, "Hearing Transcript," p. 270.

50. Ibid., p. 271.

51. Ibid., p. 274.

52. Ibid., p. 250.

53. Ibid., p. 254.

54. Perry, *Preventable Death*, p. 173.

55. During his two-year residence in Fall River for this project Dr. Perry visited each home as part of his field work and assessed hygiene on the basis of toilet facilities, density of occupation, and accessibility of sunlight.

56. Carol Aronovici, *Housing Conditions in Fall River* ([Fall River, Mass.]: Associated Charities Housing Committee, n.d.), p. 4. Report of a study commissioned by a committee of the Associated Charities of Fall River appointed December 6, 1911).

57. Ibid., p. 21.

58. Ibid., p. 8.

59. Ibid., p. 5.

60. Ibid., pp. 12–16.

61. Alice Hamilton, "Occupational Conditions and Tuberculosis," *Charities* 16 (May 15, 1906): 205; Rene and Jean Dubos, *The White Plague: Tuberculosis, Man and Society*, (Boston: Little, Brown, 1952), p. 207.

62. Hamilton, "Occupational Conditions," p. 206.

63. Perry, *Preventable Death*, p. 193; S. Lyle Cummins, *Tuberculosis in History* (London: Baillière, Tindall and Cox, 1949), p. 163.

64. Perry, *Preventable Death*, p. 118.

65. Massachusetts Commission to Investigate the Inspection of Factories, Workshops, Mercantile Establishments and Other Buildings, "Hearing Transcript," p. 268.

66. Ibid., pp. 246–47.

67. *Fall River Evening News*, January 30, 1908, p. 1.

68. *Fall River City Documents, 1911* (Fall River, Mass.: Pittman, 1912), pp. 504–05.

69. Perry, *Preventable Death*, p. 378.

70. Ibid.

71. Current practice is to calculate maternal mortality per 10,000 live births, but Perry calculated it to a base of 1,000 married women. Both methods are rough approximations, since neither is based accurately on the population at risk.

72. Louis I. Dublin, "Infant Mortality in Fall River, Massachu-

setts—A Survey of the Mortality Among 833 Infants Born in June, July and August 1913," *American Statistical Association Publications* 14 (June 1915): pp. 518–19.

73. Arnold Toynbee, *Lectures on the Industrial Revolution of the 18th Century in England* (London: Longmans, Green, 1894), p. 93.

74. William Hard, "The Law of the Killed and Wounded," *Everybody's Magazine* 19 (September 1908): 371.

75. William F. Ogburn, *Social Change* (New York: Dell, 1966), pp. 200–36.

76. Brooks Adams, *Centralization and the Law* (Boston: Little, Brown, 1906), p. 45; Harold Laski, *The State in Theory and Practice* (New York: Viking, 1945), p. 140.

77. Frederick Pollock and Frederic W. Maitland, *The History of English Law Before the Time of Edward I*, 2nd ed., vol. 2 (Cambridge: Cambridge University Press, 1898), p. 451.

78. Carl Stephenson and Frederick G. Marcham, *Sources of English Constitutional History* (New York: Harper, 1937), p. 4.

79. Massachusetts Acts and Resolves, 1911, ch. 751.

80. Oliver Wendell Holmes, *The Common Law* (Cambridge: Harvard University Press, 1967), p. 64.

81. William L. Prosser, *Handbook of the Law of Torts*, 2nd ed. (St. Paul, Minn.: West, 1955), p. 373.

82. Ibid., pp. 378, 383.

83. Henry Campbell Black, *A Law Dictionary*, 2nd ed. (St. Paul, Minn.: West, 1910), p. 810.

84. Roscoe Pound, "The Need for a Sociological Jurisprudence," *Green Bag* 19 (October 1907): 615. Fowler Harper and Fleming James, Jr., *The Law of Torts*, 2nd ed. (Boston: Little, Brown, 1956), p. 1207.

85. Eastman, *Work-Accidents*, pp. 183, 187.

86. Parry, *The Law and the Poor*, pp. 79–80.

87. Leonard W. Levy, *The Law of the Commonwealth and Chief Justice Shaw* (Cambridge: Harvard University Press, 1957), p. 170.

88. Ibid., pp. 166, 169.

89. C. B. Labatt, *Commentaries on the Law of Masters and Servants* (Rochester, N.Y.: Lawyers' Cooperative Publishing Co., 1904), p. 167.

90. Harper and James, *The Law of Torts*, p. 1163.

91. Labatt, *Law of Masters and Servants*, pp. 1039, 1082.

92. Ibid., pp. 725–27.

93. Ibid., p. 695.

94. Ibid., p. 156.

95. Prosser, *The Law of Torts*, p. 313.

96. Labatt, *Law of Masters and Servants*, p. 156.

97. Ibid., p. 62n.

98. Ibid., pp. 157, 694.

99. Ibid., p. 164.

100. Bradley, J., Tuttle v. Detroit, Grand Haven and Milwaukee Ry., 122 US 189 7 Sup Ct 1166, 30 L. Ed. 1114 (1887); Black, J., Tiller v. Atlantic Coast Line Ry. Co., 318 US 54, 59, 63 Sup Ct 444, 87 L. Ed. 610 (1943).

101. Massachusetts Acts and Resolves, 1887, ch. 270.

102. Harry Weiss, "Employers' Liability and Workmen's Compensation," in John R. Commons, et al., eds., *History of Labor in the United States, 1896–1932*, vol. 3 (New York: Macmillan, 1935), p. 573.

103. George Sutherland, "Employers' Liability and Workmen's Compensation," *Independent* 72 (May 9, 1912): 1007.

104. Eastman, *Work-Accidents*, p. 188.

105. Hard, "Law of the Killed and Wounded," p. 369.

106. Roger S. Warner, "Employers' Liability as an Industrial Problem," *The Green Bag* 18 (April 1906): 190.

107. Jerold S. Auerbach, *Unequal Justice* (New York: Oxford University Press, 1976), p. 45.

108. Ralph H. Blanchard, *Liability and Compensation Insurance* (New York: Appleton, 1917), p. 62.

109. Auerbach, *Unequal Justice*, p. 45.

CHAPTER 3

1. Lyman Mills Papers, vol. LAC2, Baker Library, Harvard University, Cambridge, Mass.

2. Lyman Mills Papers, vol. PH17.

3. Lyman Mills Papers, vols. LAC1 to LAC13 (injury reports) and vols. PH1 to PH20 (correspondence) were the primary source of data. Payrolls from 1895 to 1910 were sampled to calculate departmental sex ratios. Professor Robert G. Layer's work sheets on textile payrolls were also helpful.

4. Massachusetts Acts and Resolves, 1877, ch. 214.

5. Lyman Mills Papers, vol. ED1; Dwight Manufacturing Papers, vol. DN10 (also in Baker Library, Harvard University. Cambridge, Mass.).

6. Massachusetts State Board of Health, *Thirty-Eighth Annual Report* (Boston: Wright and Potter, 1907), pp. 477–80.

7. Frederick L. Hoffman, "Industrial Accidents," *Bulletin of the Bureau of Labor*, No. 78 (Washington, D.C.: Government Printing Office, 1908), pp. 431–33.

8. The proportion unable to speak English in the Lyman work force as a whole is not known. Among injured workers *not* taxed for carelessness, 71 percent spoke English, while among those defined as careless, 39 percent spoke English. Among the injured group as a whole, 52 percent were English speakers.

9. Massachusetts Acts and Resolves, 1887, ch. 270.

10. Massachusetts Acts and Resolves, 1911, ch. 751.

CHAPTER 4

1. Dwight Manufacturing Company Papers, Baker Library, Harvard University, Cambridge, Mass. Agent (plant manager) to Insurer, vol. HL2, 3/17/02. Agent to Insurer letters are in volumes HL1 to HL4 and Insurer to Agent letters in ML30 to ML44. Hereafter cited by volume and date in parentheses in the text.

2. Talcott Parsons, *The Social System* (New York: Free Press, 1964), p. 313.

3. Massachusetts Industrial Accident Board, *Third Annual Report* (Boston: Wright and Potter, 1916), p. 76.

4. American Mutual Liability Insurance to Samuel Ames, 3/31/94 and 4/3/94 in Samuel Ames Papers, Rhode Island Historical Society, Providence, R.I.

5. See Jerold S. Auerbach, *Unequal Justice* (New York: Oxford University Press, 1976), pp. 43–50.

6. Hamilton Manufacturing Collection, vol. 113, 5/12/90, in Baker Library, Harvard University, Cambridge, Mass. Hereafter cited by volume and date in parentheses in the text.

7. Lawrence Manufacturing Company Collection, vol. GO2, 8/26/92 and 11/8/92, in Baker Library, Harvard University, Cambridge, Mass. Hereafter cited by volume and date in parentheses in the text.

8. Lowell Hospital Register, 9/24/99 to 11/10/05 in St. Joseph's Hospital, Lowell, Mass.

CHAPTER 5

1. Ralph H. Blanchard, *Liability and Compensation Insurance* (New York: Appleton, 1917), p. 36.

2. Wolfgang Friedman, *Law in a Changing Society* (New York: Columbia University Press, 1972), p. 163.

3. I. M. Rubinow, *Social Insurance* (New York: Holt, 1913), p. 163, 168.

4. Roy Lubove, *The Struggle for Social Security, 1900–1935* (Cambridge: Harvard University Press, 1968), p. 57.

5. James Weinstein, *The Corporate Ideal and the Liberal State* (Boston: Beacon Press, 1968), p. 43.

6. Robert Asher, "Business and Workers' Welfare in the Progressive Era: Workmen's Compensation Reform in Massachusetts, 1880–1911," *Business History Review* 43 (Winter 1969): 454.

7. Weinstein, *Corporate Ideal*, pp. 46–47.

8. Robert Asher, "The 1911 Wisconsin Workmen's Compensation Law: A Study in Conservative Labor Reform," *Wisconsin Magazine of History* 57 (Winter 1973–74): 126–27.

9. Irwin Yellowitz, *Labor and the Progressive Movement in New York State, 1897–1916* (Ithaca, N.Y.: Cornell University Press, 1965), p. 110.

10. James Parker Hall, "The New York Workmen's Compensation Act Decision," *Journal of Political Economy* 19 (October 1911): 694ff.

11. Theodore Roosevelt to Hiram Johnson, October 27, 1911, in *The Letters of Theodore Roosevelt*, vol. 7, ed. E. E. Morrison, (Cambridge: Harvard University Press, 1954), p. 421.

12. Morris Cohen, *Law and the Social Order* (Hamden, Conn.: Archon, 1967), p. 127.

13. Prosser, *Torts*, p. 384 (see n. 81, p. 151).

14. H. M. Somers and A. R. Somers, *Workmen's Compensation* (New York: Wiley, 1954), p. 268.

15. Lubove, *Struggle for Social Security*, pp. 57–59.

16. E. H. Downey, "The Present Status of Workmen's Compensation in the United States," *American Economic Review* 12 (March 1922): 131.

17. Somers, *Workmen's Compensation*, p. 269.

18. Walter S. Nichols, "An Argument Against Liability," *Annals of the American Academy of Political and Social Science* 38 (July 1911): 159, 161.

19. Ibid., 163.

20. Frank Lewis, "Employers' Liability," *Atlantic Monthly* 103 (January 1909): 60.

21. William J. McGill, "Litigation-Prone Society," *New York State Journal of Medicine* 78 (March 1978): 661.

22. James MacGregor Burns, *Roosevelt: The Lion and the Fox* (New York: Harcourt, Brace, 1956), pp. 180–81.

23. 48 U.S. Statutes 195.

24. Richard C. Cortner, *Wagner Act Cases* (Knoxville: University of Tennessee Press, 1964), p. 62.

25. *The Statesman's Book of John of Salisbury*, trans. John Dickinson (New York: Russell and Russell, 1963), p. 64ff; James Madison, Federalist No. 10, in *Federalist Papers*, (New York: New American Library, 1961), pp. 77–84.

26. Rolf Dahrendorf, *Class and Class Conflict in Industrial Society* (Stanford: Stanford University Press, 1959), pp. 225–27.

27. Philip Ross, *The Government as a Source of Union Power* (Providence, R.I.: Brown University Press, 1965), p. 70.

28. Ibid., pp. 259.

29. Harry A. Mills and Emily Clark Brown, *From the Wagner Act to Taft-Hartley* (Chicago: University of Chicago Press, 1950), pp. 363, 370, 390, 391.

30. Nicholas Askounes Ashford, *Crisis in the Workplace: Occupational Disease and Injury* (Cambridge: MIT Press, 1976), p. 190.

31. 61LRRM1073

32. Bureau of National Affairs, *The Job Safety and Health Act of 1970* (Washington, D.C.: Bureau of National Affairs, 1971), p. 17.

33. U.S., Congress, Senate, Committee on Labor and Public Wel-

fare, *Hearings on S. 2864* (Washington, D.C.: Government Printing Office, 1968), p. 62.

34. 84 U.S. Statutes 1590.

35. See Bureau of National Affairs, *Job Safety and Health Act of 1970* (Washington, D.C.: Bureau of National Affairs, 1971), pp. 13–21; Page and O'Brien, *Bitter Wages*, pp. 161–91; Ashford, *Crisis in the Workplace*, pp. 52–57.

36. Ashford, *Crisis in the Workplace*, p. 199.

CHAPTER 6

1. Somers, *Workmen's Compensation*, p. 142.

2. Ibid., p. 156.

3. *Report of the National Commission on State Workmen's Compensation Laws* (Washington, D.C.: Government Printing Office, 1972), p. 107.

4. John H. Lewis, "A Workmen's Restoration System," in *Supplemental Studies for the National Commission on State Workmen's Compensation Laws*, vol. 3, (Washington, D.C.: Government Printing Office, 1973), p. 512.

5. Ibid., p. 516.

6. Marcus Rosenblum, ed., *Compendium on Workmen's Compensation* (Washington, D.C.: Government Printing Office, 1973), p. 205.

7. Benjamin Marcus, "Advocating the Rights of the Injured," in Earl F. Cheit and Margaret S. Gordon, eds., *Occupational Disability and Public Policy* (New York: Wiley, 1963), p. 79.

8. Ibid., p. 82.

9. *Providence Evening Bulletin*, July 7, 1977, p. 1.

10. Robert L. Caleo, "Absenteeism," *Administrative Management* 24 (June 1962): 245.

11. John Collie, *Malingering and Feigned Sickness* (London: Arnold, 1913), p. 1.

12. Ibid., pp. 10–11.

13. Ray Davidson, *Peril on the Job* (Washington, D.C.: Public Affairs Press, 1970), p. 143.

14. Collie, *Malingering*, p. 11.

15. Philip Powell *et al.*, *2,000 Accidents* (London: National Institute of Industrial Psychology, 1971), pp. 28–29.

16. Davidson, *Peril*, p. 138.

17. U.S. Department of Labor, Bureau of Labor Statistics, *Major Collective Bargaining Agreements: Safety and Health Provisions*, Bulletin 1425–16 (Washington, D.C.: Government Printing Office, 1976), pp. 19–20.

18. Correspondence from Oil, Chemical and Atomic Workers Union, Bethlehem Steel Corporation, Republic Steel Corporation, General Motors Corporation, Firestone Tire and Rubber Company, and United Rubber Workers Union Local 5.

19. Consolidated Edison Company of New York, Turkus, 61LA607 (1973).

20. Budd Company, Jaffee, 17LA911 (1951).

21. United States Steel, Dybeck, 56LA769 (1971).

22. Blaw Knox Company, Teple, 58LA571 (1972).

23. Hegeler Zinc Co., Elson, 8LA571 (1972).

24. *National Bituminous Coal Wage Agreement of 1974*, pp. 8–9.

25. Melvin A. Glassner, "Commentary: Occupational Safety and Health–A Labor View," *Wayne State Law Review* 20 (July 1974): 992.

26. United States Steel, Dybeck, 60LA258 (1972).

27. Paragon Bridge and Steel Co., Gross, 42LA339 (1964).

28. *New York Times*, February 2, 1977, sec. 1, p. 41.

29. *New York Times*, January 23, 1977, sec. 1, p. 12.

30. *New York Times*, June 6, 1976, sec. 3, p. 1.

31. This account is based upon the following sources: State of New Hampshire Department of Health and Welfare, Certificate of Death of Jose Salazar Ramirez aka Guadalupe, May 11, 1976; State of New Hampshire Department of Labor, Employer's First Report of Injury or Occupational Disease of Jose Guadalupe, May 11, 1976; "Suncook Worker killed in Machine," *Concord Monitor*, May 11, 1976; "OSHA Finds Violation at Hodgson," *Concord Monitor*, May 21, 1976; letter from Robert Duvall, April 14, 1977; Occupational Safety and Health Review Commission Case File 76-2613 supplied by Manchester, N.H. area office of OSHA.

32. Dan Smoot, *The Business End of Government* (Belmont, Mass.: Western Island, 1973), p. 55.

33. Albert Costain, quoted in Patrick Kinnersley, *The Hazards of Work: How to Fight Them* (London: Pluto, 1974), p. 14.

34. U.S. Department of Labor, Occupational Safety and Health Administration, Case File 3-D-6600-77-6.

35. OSHA, Case File 3-D-2060-76-54.

36. Rachel Scott, *Muscle and Blood* (New York: Dutton, 1974), p. 287.

37. Leonard Woodcock, *The Unfulfilled Promise of OSHA* (Detroit: United Automobile Workers, 1975), p. 4.

38. Joseph A. Page and Peter N. Munsing, "Occupational Health and the Federal Government: The Wages Are Still Bitter," *Law and Contemporary Problems* 38 (1974): 666–67.

39. "Job Safety and Health: Inadequate Enforcement and Stalled Review," (Washington, D.C.: Health Research Group, n.d.), p. 1.

40. Ibid., p. 3.

41. *Dan Smoot Report*, February 7, 1973 and February 28, 1973.

42. Smoot, *Business End of Government*, pp. 48, 53.

43. Statement before House Select Subcommittee on Labor by E. Stanley Rittenhouse, February 25, 1975.

44. Alan Stang, "OSHTAPO: Warning—It's Against the Law to Have an Accident," *American Opinion* (October 1975): 3–4.

45. OSHC 1451 at 1459–60.

46. 48 LW 5022 at 5044.

47. Ibid. (emphasis supplied).

48. 48 LW 5022 at 5053.

49. Quoted in *What Every UAW Representative Should Know About Health and Safety* (Detroit: United Automobile Workers, 1979), p. 17.

50. Alvin Gouldner, *The Coming Crisis of Western Sociology* (New York: Basic Books, 1970), p. 304.

51. Quoted in Richard Severo, "Too Hot to Handle," *New York Times Magazine*, April 10, 1977, p. 36.

Index